Also by Martin E. Marty
Politics, Religion, and the Common Good

Education, Religion, and the Common Good

Martin E. Marty
with Jonathan Moore

Education, Religion, and the Common Good

Advancing a Distinctly American
Conversation About Religion's
Role in Our Shared Life

JOSSEY-BASS
A Wiley Company
San Francisco

Jossey-Bass books and products are available through most bookstores. To contact Jossey-Bass directly, call (888) 378-2537, fax to (800) 605-2665, or visit our website at www.josseybass.com.

Substantial discounts on bulk quantities of Jossey-Bass books are available to corporations, professional associations, and other organizations. For details and discount information, contact the special sales department at Jossey-Bass.

Manufactured in the United States of America on Lyons Falls Turin Book. This paper is acid-free and 100 percent totally chlorine-free.

Library of Congress Cataloging-in-Publication Data

Marty, Martin E., date
    Education, religion, and the common good: advancing a
distinctly American conversation about religion's role in our
shared life / Martin E. Marty with Jonathan Moore.—1st ed.
        p. cm.
    Includes bibliographical references and index.
    ISBN 0-7879-5033-5 (alk. paper)
    1. Religion in the public schools—United States. 2. Universities and colleges—United States—Religion. 3. Church and education—United States. I. Moore, Jonathan, date. II.
    Title.
    LC111 .M32 2000
    379.2'8'0973—dc21   00-09152

FIRST EDITION
HB Printing   10 9 8 7 6 5 4 3 2 1

Contents

Education, Religion, and the Common Good

Introduction

Why Read This Book?

E ach of us leads a seamless life, a life that flows through various stages from infancy to old age. At each of those stages, some form of religion and many forms of education—whether thanks to schooling or the experience of hard knocks—make up part of our experience.

Experts, because they specialize—the fields of kindergarten and graduate school education differ, for instance—often give the impression that the seamless life can be snipped up and fragmented. This book, however, sets out to weave together the various education specialties as it keeps an eye on the various passages of life. To my knowledge, no other book yet exists that similarly connects concerns of elementary, high school, college or university, and graduate school in respect to the twin dimensions I seek to explore here: education and religion.

What has provoked this seamless or holistic approach is concern for the "common good." Helping produce citizens whose lives, through their stages and specialties, display a sense of connectedness contributes to a society that while ensuring individual freedom also calls people to seek common ground so that they can deal with personal and public issues more creatively.

I further believe that every author should be clear about what makes a book distinctive. In a world full of already crowded libraries, each new work has to make a case for its existence. If readers can get the same thing more conveniently or less expensively somewhere else, they will go elsewhere. But if readers sense that a particular book offers something vital and singular, they will find strong reasons to consult it.

This book, I believe, is distinctive. Granted, libraries have thousands, even tens of thousands of different books on education and religion. There are thousands more on religious education, educating for religion. And if my computer searches and bibliographic studies are accurate, hundreds of valid and valuable books have already connected education and religion on some level or other. So why does this one deserve attention?

The mention of levels begins to reveal this book's distinctive contribution. Like so many areas of modern life, both education and religion are full of differentiation and specialization. Topics are chopped up and divided, as they usually must be if we are to understand them. So specialists in elementary education concern themselves with its world, but they only occasionally and probably casually glance at issues in higher education. Likewise, higher education also has its own set of specialties. True, those in higher education, it is said, have at least one thing in common: a grievance over the parking situation. And most of them probably read the *Chronicle of Higher Education*. But liberal arts colleges are on one track and private universities are on another. Private and public universities and their personnel and supporters often have separate interests. All these schools get divided into departments, disciplines, and specialties. Faculties and student bodies become interest groups, providers, and customers of many competing sorts.

With these realities, it is no wonder that higher educators generally lack interest in elementary and secondary education. As parents, they will care about the private and public schools their children attend. Many are responsible citizens and will take a turn on the school board. Some will teach in specialties that train teachers for the young. Not a few will complain about the bad products that secondary schools produce. But to find higher educators reading books on kindergarten life is as rare as having middle school teachers writing master's theses on graduate education. All these are in separate boxes or on differing tracks.

This book attempts to unite their common concerns around a single issue: religion. Religion itself is also differentiated. Most citizens specialize in at most one faith: their own or the one they have chosen to reject and oppose. Those of ecumenical and interreligious curiosity may try to learn more, but after realizing that there are more than twenty-five thousand separate Christian groups in the world—to say nothing of other faiths—they may quickly lose heart.

Can one interest a Unitarian-Universalist kindergarten teacher in Boston in questions of religion at the University of Notre Dame, and vice versa? Do Mormons in Utah (other than dissertation writers) have a good excuse to examine United Methodism in Georgia? Do pastors, theologians, chaplains, and caregivers find much in common beyond what their specialty demands? Not likely. Theorists have their theories and do not always find them coinciding. Practitioners have their practices and pursue them independently, with little evident curiosity about others unless they are direct competitors.

Given the fragmented nature of this audience, it is not surprising that bibliographic searches reveal plenty of good, specialized writings on religion and education. What distinguishes this book, I hope, is that it resists this compartmentalization. Instead of dealing with education on one level or another, this book calls on readers to reflect on all levels. It also resists focusing on one faith community in some specialized way. Instead, it attempts to interest people as citizens—believers or not—in religion and education in more general, coordinating, integrative ways.

I have at least three sets of readers in mind, and I hope that all will read the entire book. First, there are those of you who despise most outcroppings of spirituality and religion and may read these pages in order to learn the enemy's plans. However, you will not be able to set up the best defense by dealing only with one level of education, whether kindergarten or postdoctoral studies. A second group of readers includes those of you who believe that there can be a potentially healthy relationship between religion and education. You, too, will achieve little by reforming thinking only about early grades or higher education. Finally, a last group of readers may be most interested in private and parochial schooling. But again, I submit that advocates can only fully attend to the complexities of extrapublic education by faithfully attending to issues in public education as well. Private and parochial schooling, at the very least, must be seen as "out there" in public. More important, education at the parochial level is much involved with the public. Teachers ordinarily have to be certified by public accrediting agencies, and in most instances, private curricula must meet public standards. Recall also that such schools receive the public benefits of fire and police protection, at public expense. If affiliated with religious institutions, private schools benefit from tax exemptions. This means that although such schools may be serving all taxpayers by relieving pressure on public school rosters, they are at the same time being supported by people who pay higher taxes because parochial schools pay no property taxes. Mention taxing policies and you have trouble escaping the public dimensions of private and parochial education.

To make the case for an integrative approach more concrete, let's look at an illustrative example: the issue of *school vouchers*. What light do we throw on the subject by treating it seamlessly? Vouchers imply a system that involves some sort of tax support or relief for parents who opt to send their children to private or parochial schools. But looked at from a perspective that accounts for the interrelated nature of educational levels, a gap in logic begins to appear.

Let's refer to this cognitive disjunction as the Grade Thirteen Principle. The argument behind it: one year after high school—

grade thirteen—policies related to private education that were once ruled out are now often ruled back in.

Here's how it works. In many states, the equivalent of a voucher system already operates. Individuals or families that choose private and even church-related colleges can often get a measure of tax relief to defray tuition costs. The more radical church-state separationists may oppose this practice on principled grounds, and some state university advocates may grumble because tax relief may level the playing field between private and tax-supported schools. But aside from these small minorities, any objection to this common practice is rare and faint.

Now step back just a year: from grade twelve on down, envision the same individuals positioned to attend parochial schools. To offer tax relief to those who opt for private education is suddenly controversial. Suggesting such a policy raises red flags from legislatures to school accrediting agencies to other interest groups.

The point is that generally speaking, the public's logic is elusive. Why favor tax breaks for one set of students but not for the other? Perhaps it has something to do with concerns over the quality and finances of public education. But most arguments remain unconvincing, because the same logic could be applied to higher education; in either case, public institutions lose every tax dollar that goes instead to private schools.

Another example that demonstrates the value of an integrative approach concerns *religious studies programs*. As with school vouchers, the debate over having religion in the curriculum follows the Grade Thirteen Principle. In higher education, the credible case has been made that even tax-supported institutions should include religious studies programs. Having separate religion programs or departments helps round out for college students an accurate, realistic picture of the world.

The same, of course, can be argued for lower educational levels. After all, how can third graders, no less than university students,

gain an accurate perspective on their surroundings without somehow being introduced to the religious dimension? Here, however,
things become tricky. Having religion in the university curriculum
assumes that students have the critical skills necessary to digest and
evaluate the material presented to them. Presumably, they can dis-
tinguish between mastering the material and being converted by it
and have the freedom to make informed choices about belief. In primary and secondary education, however, this assumption obviously
does not hold, especially for children in the lower grades. Moreover,
grades twelve and below are not quite so divided into separate disciplines presided over by specialists, thus making a kind of broad-
based religion curriculum more difficult to install. Where should
religion come up? In history? Science? Arts and literature? None or
all of the above?

There are more instances of the Grade Thirteen Principle at
work. For example, it is relatively uncontroversial for State U's glee
club or madrigal group to sing great religious choral music, but it is
often quite controversial for a high school chorus to undertake a similar effort. These issues are complicated, to be sure. When is it inconsistent to apply the Grade Thirteen Principle, and when is it not?

To aim at all levels and more general ways might be a recipe for
superficiality, a once-over-lightly view of the issues. Only you, the
reader, can judge if the book has successfully avoided this hazard.
But I think it is worth the risk. Amid and among the many books
on education and religion, this one is to my knowledge the only one
that deals with all levels and in general religious terms with the
common good. That provides the prism and perspective. It is this
theme that helped me sort out what material to include or exclude,
and I hope this focus serves you well in the chapters to come.

1

Just What Are We
Talking About, Anyway?

I don't want to take up too much time with lengthy definitions. However, readers have a right to know exactly what I mean by specific important terms. In addition to referring to *common good*, I will also be making frequent mention of *education*, *religion*, and the art of *conversation*. Let's run through these terms so that we're all on the same page.

The Common Good

In this book, *common good* refers to the good of the larger public. The common good is the goal sought by citizens across the personal boundaries of religion, race, philosophy, taste, and commitment. In other words, the common good transcends individual interests. That good may include moral, civil, aesthetic, and spiritual elements. For example, I will argue that helping high schoolers understand religion and religions is not a task that only religious leaders and educators should care about for religious reasons. If educators aspire to teach a fairly accurate picture of the world around us, it is both necessary and good to have religious themes included in secondary education. Also, if we assume that it is unfair to "establish," privilege, demean, or minimize particular faiths, then the common good is furthered only by fair-minded, unprejudiced teaching about religion and religions.

Education

We can define *education* rather briskly here. There are many books on educational theory and practice, and the authors of these certainly connect education with its Latin root, *educere*, "to lead out," as if to draw out of a child and enlarge on what is already there. Some specialized education does that, but most educators do not get up in the morning and start thinking about how to *educe* or "draw out" what is there. They will instead concentrate on lesson plans or lab assignments. They might even try to *induce* ("lead in") new learning using information not yet "there."

In this book, the meaning of *education* usually comes closest to "schooling." Although schooling includes rich varieties—home, parochial, public, private, collegiate—that term does at least bring some focus. So unless otherwise noted, in this conversation we will picture education as something that is transacted in institutions—kindergartens, homes, churches, graduate universities, church-related colleges, high schools, and the like. What goes on in those institutions includes imparting information, nurturing personal and social growth, stimulating curiosity, increasing awareness, acquiring practical skills, focusing the critical faculties, developing means to test reality, and inculcating wisdom. The best advice: when in doubt, think of *education* and *schooling* as synonymous. That way we can keep focus and do a bit of narrowing.

Religion

For thirty-five years, I taught at the University of Chicago, in a neighborhood that had attracted half a dozen theological schools. Someone once assessed that if all these libraries counted their religious holdings, there would be more than 1.3 million books within a half mile of each other. Similarly sized collections are at Harvard or Yale, and all three of these would not cover all the religion titles found in European and Asian libraries. Some cataloguer somewhere had to determine that such books belonged to the generic category "religion." Many of those authors took great pains to define religion, and it is mind-boggling to think of boiling all that down to a workable definition for this book.

Sometimes, when in a puckish mood, I give a standard answer when asked to define religion. I relate that for some years I was one of eight editors who had to meet regularly to decide what topics, themes, and categories belonged in a fifteen-volume work called *The Encyclopedia of Religion*. What is religion? It's the kind of stuff you put in a book with that title.

Here, as with education, there has to be some delimiting. Almost anything can have a religious dimension should we wish to find it—professional football, beauty contests, astrology, dieting, and all the rest. But this is much too broad: if everything is religious, then nothing is religious. Yet an accurate definition of religion should not be confined only to what we find in the "Churches and Synagogues" section of the Yellow Pages. We cannot neatly confine our curiosities about religion to the institutional, as we have done with education, though we shall often keep religious institutions in mind. Certainly for most citizens, most educators, and most judges, religion in its institutional form is most related to problems concerning education and the common good. But the line gets blurry. Many people today disdain organized or institutional religion in favor of an individualized spirituality. They, too, will soon find that even this kind of religion raises public issues for education as well.

We can say a few more things about defining religion. Not a lexicographer or a philosopher, I shall do what historians tend to do: look at what everyone describes as "religious" and see what features it has. In doing so, one finds four or five of the following characteristics present in most phenomena called "religious."

Ultimate Concern

What do you finally live by? For what would you be willing to die? For you, what is the Big Deal, the Whole Ball of Wax? What guiding principle organizes and infuses your life with meaning? The answer is your ultimate concern. It may or may not relate to God or gods. By itself it is not necessarily religion, but all religions will make metaphysical claims about the nature and purpose of reality. The most important of these claims corresponds to one's ultimate concern.

Community

Through history and ordinarily in our own time, in the name of some ultimate concern people gather together to check out signals with each other, fortify each other, ward off common foes, celebrate, or mourn. There certainly are exceptions, especially today, where spirituality often moves independently of groups, but most religious people continue to relate in some way to a community.

Myth and Symbol

Myth here does not indicate something false; rather it refers to modes of communicating and believing through stylized narratives. Symbol does not mean that one "merely" finds an image, metaphor, or sign to stand for something else. It does mean that the religious person does not like flat, reductive, matter-of-fact communication when more memorable, evocative forms are present. Myths and symbols relate religious truths in creative, often artistic ways.

Rite and Ceremony

Of course, some religious acts are spontaneous, singular, and unre-peatable. But we tend to notice something as religious when groups choose to do the same thing to people at the same age: initiation, adolescence, marriage, death. Religious people also mark seasons, holidays, and other particular occasions with other rites and cere-monies. These actions help identify and clarify the boundaries of religious communities.

Behavioral Correlates

You do not have to be religious to work out patterns of behavior. We all acquire and adopt habits, customs, manners, and works that have few religious connotations. But if you are religious, you will almost certainly relate in some way to codes of conduct and stipulations that demand responses. Most religions map out for followers what virtues are most important and what actions are or are not acceptable. These behaviors, like rites and ceremonies, further clarify the core identity of religious groups.

Discussing Education, Religion, and the Common Good: Models for Dialogue

Now that we have some general understanding of our key terms, it's time to begin talking about how education and religion relate to the common good. But how are we going to talk? After all, these topics can be combustible. What's going to prevent any discussion of these issues from degenerating into a shouting match? When nothing less than the common good is at stake, we want discussions to generate more light than heat. In order to do that, let's look at two possible avenues for debating these issues: argument and conversation.

Argument

An *argument* is what usually goes on when people come anywhere close to topics such as religion and education. When people argue, they usually hold strong positions from which they often attack, or defend against, those who disagree. Since argument usually concerns problems, arguers often have in mind answers and solutions. Whether we win arguments or lose them, most of us would readily agree that argument is necessary for humanity's progress.

We argue not only with family members, neighbors, other citizens, and public figures, but also sometimes with ourselves. With ourselves? Yes, on occasion, when we feel sure of a position, only to find it challenged so effectively that we must rethink it. We marshal the ideas attached to that position, and then from another corner of the brain, we bring out new data, new suggestions. A little war goes on in the mind, and we see the need to settle the issue one way or another.

For instance, many citizens find themselves conflicted and unsettled over the issue of school vouchers. The argument within the mind for them begins with the responsible citizen taking stock of existing ideas and commitments. Suppose that you, like most Americans, support public elementary and high schools. Such taxpayer-supported schools have provided broad opportunities for children to gain knowledge and acquire skills to last a lifetime. You recognize that for all their faults, the public schools continue to help children of immigrants from all over the globe become part of some common American culture. It has become fashionable to knock these schools, to find fault with almost all dimensions of their assignments and roles. Yet notwithstanding their flaws, we are used to public schools. We cannot picture American life without them. Indeed, much of their strength lies in the fact that they tend to be local institutions where ordinary people have some say.

So with those assumptions in mind, you are ready to engage the issue further. Here enters the factor that many private alternatives to public schools have religious affiliations. No matter where Americans stand in this debate, most of them agree that church and state somehow relate to each other and need some protection from each other. But what forms should this relationship take in matters of education? How much and what kind of protection do religion and government need? What does the Constitution require?

As this relates to education, we can turn to history for some help. Americans have a long tradition on which to draw for ensuring the public character of education. Though we shall forever argue about how to apply its terms, we have inherited and cherish a national constitution. It anticipates some of our most important civic issues and helps frame others, including education and religion.

Perhaps most obviously, there is the First Amendment: "Congress shall make no law respecting an establishment of religion, or prohibiting the free exercise thereof." These words help carve out the zone in which public schools operate. Some Americans, using the language of Thomas Jefferson, argue that the First Amendment erected a "wall of separation" between church and state. Here "state" refers to the people responsible for education. That wall allows no contact between religion and public education.

Jefferson may have had his wall, but fellow founder James Madison spoke instead of a "line of distinction" between civil and religious authorities. Thinkers who line up behind Madison contend that Jefferson's wall is an unofficial and inappropriate metaphor and that any boundary between religion and education should be understood as wavy and permeable.

Often all sides try to use the language of the First Amendment against their opponents. Arguers often invoke the First Amendment's *establishment* clause ("Congress shall make no law respecting an establishment of religion") or the *free exercise* clause ("or prohibiting the free exercise thereof"). Supporters of a strict understanding of the prohibition against establishment argue that there can be no relationship between government and religion. Not only is it unjust and unconstitutional to force citizens to subsidize religions in which they do not believe, but both religion and government are corrupted by any financial relationship between the two. The Constitution requires each to stand on its own, they contend; making room for religion in taxpayer-funded and government-run public education violates that requirement.

By contrast, some people use the free exercise clause to argue that religion should be kept separate from public education. Madison's line of distinction must remain between the two lest government be tempted to dictate or distort religious ideas and values. Better to keep the two separate so that the exercise of religion, in whatever form, remains truly free.

Challenges also come from other citizens, religious groups, school leaders, interest groups, and the courts. All raise difficult and important questions. Have the public schools been all that effective at introducing the appropriate ways to behave in civil society? Or do the schools continue to educate students in such a way that minimizes, overlooks, or demeans the unavoidably religious dimensions of human life?

Other claims follow. Do public schools do a good job of integrating children of diverse backgrounds into a common American culture? Schools tend to reflect local conditions, following residential patterns, and hence are often segregated along lines of race and class. For a better model, perhaps we should take a look at parochial schools, which draw students from different neighborhoods and where races more freely intermix. With this evidence, who can say that public schools somehow do a better job of creating good citizens than private and parochial schools?

The questions continue to pile up. Many parents, especially those from clearly defined religious traditions and communities, argue that the public schools teach a generalized form of religion. Is it fair or constitutional, they ask, for them to pay taxes in support of "secular humanism," "democracy," or other worldviews that contradict or undercut their own? If they want to protect their children from that generalized religion, whatever it might be, parents must send them to private or parochial schools. Doesn't this represent an unfair system of double taxation, they ask? Why should we have to pay taxes toward a public education system from which we derive no benefits? To make things fair, these parents argue for tuition vouchers that allow everyone the freedom to choose their own schools. And by the way, they add, won't placing all schools on equal footing create a climate of competition that will ensure that schools improve? What, after all, could be more American than an educational free market?

We've only begun to touch on the complexities of the issues surrounding religion and education. Certainly these issues will continue to trouble citizens, both locally and nationally, for years to come. Both voters and courts will be required to wrestle with school vouchers and similar programs. No matter what the outcome, many citizens will be unhappy. How can we keep those unsatisfied citizens from withdrawing into circles where resentment builds and sniping begins? How can we keep all parties, not just the winners, from abandoning the search for the common good?

From Argument to Conversation

You will have misread the book's purpose if you think that I'm suggesting that conversation can replace argument. In the end, courts have to decide issues, and we are all in trouble if judges do not hear arguments, ponder them, and then argue among themselves. Interest groups—whether Presbyterian, atheist, creationist, union-affiliated, ethnic, or class-based—have a right to be heard. And for the common good, these groups need to be heard. Because many of their interests will clash, we need argument. No matter how distasteful we sometimes find it, argument in legislatures and courts is necessary for an effective public order.

When contentious issues are in the air, citizens naturally choose sides. They line up the armament of their arguments and fire away. Often their shooting is so noisy that they cannot hear one another. But some combatants may tire of such a battle, lay down arms, and begin to listen to what opponents have to say. That listening begins to shape and change what goes on in their own minds. That listening may alter what happens at the school board meeting or in the voting booth. Some, weary of warfare, may begin to wonder, isn't there a better way to engage issues passionately than endlessly to hurl argument against argument, returning fire with fire?

One alternative to a rhetorical war of attrition and unending battle is *conversation*. Opponents can step back a bit and, without tossing away their arsenal of answers, start making more of questions. This is the essence of conversation: participants allow the *question* to guide them. Unlike a heated argument, conversation can be freer, sometimes almost playful. Combatants can let down their guard, meet the other, and begin to listen. Constructive responses often follow: "Until I met you and we began conversing, I never thought of your position that way." "I think you have a point, too. But I really wonder if . . ." You can fill in the blank from there. Conversations, guided by questions, usually surprise us as they carry us in unexpected directions.

For that argument to be enriched and nuanced, however, it needs refreshment. Listening to the other—conversing—is one of the best ways to deepen and broaden public discussion. That's why this book is dedicated to fueling a conversation about education, religion, and the common good.

Our Own Conversations

The argument for conversation—yes, argument, because we're defending a position—grows out of a long record and recent interest in conversation as an instrument to advance the common good.

For the historical part, I recall on occasion sitting in the circle of advisers to the late Martin Luther King Jr. when he was seeking change in Chicago. It was easy for King, his associates, and all civil rights supporters to bring forth arguments, defend answers, and attack others with different answers. Integrationists could explain how present policies contradicted themes in both the Declaration of Independence and the U.S. Constitution. To the large majority of citizens who belonged to the biblical tradition, civil rights proponents could bring forth arguments from the prophets, from the Gospels, and from the religious traditions to which Americans were committed.

They also knew the limits of argument. When you and I argue, one of us must either win or lose. One of us must triumph, while the other might be driven away—or, on occasion, be convinced to switch positions. (Conversation differs here: no one ever says, "I won that conversation.") To truly change people, King and his advisers knew they had to come at issues a different way.

I kept hearing one of his lieutenants constantly talk of "incubating" so that people would change their ideas, beliefs, and actions. What did he mean? How did this incubating work? People interested in the mechanics of conversation can learn much from King's deputy. "Here's how it works," he said. "You get a great big hall. You invite as many and as many kinds of people as you have room for. You hope they jam the place. Then before you shut the door, you say, 'Don't any of you come out until you have the answer.' And they will always ask, 'Well, what is the question? What is the problem?' And we tell them, 'Just start talking, and you will find out what the problem is.'"

For all the simplicity of that technique, and for all the chaos we can easily imagine if something goes a bit wrong, there is much to recommend that approach. The King aide did not have a naive faith in human goodness or intelligence. He was not writing off the value of experts—he *was* an expert. But he trusted the experience people would bring to conversation about problems. He had to know that a good deal of posturing, bickering, and self-centeredness could restrict the conversation's agenda. And he knew he could not know exactly what topic the conversation would address. But he trusted a group to formulate priorities; he knew that leadership would get some fresh perspectives and new agenda items. In short, King's associate trusted in the promise of conversation.

Some of us tried this kind of thing in public housing during the time following King's death. More militant black separatists, often inspired by radical versions of Black Power, started providing their own agendas. They served notice that black consciousness was radicalizing all blacks, and a race war might well impend. These militants produced manifestos, made demands, declared ideologies, and often provoked backlash. Moderate African Americans and whites in general began to feel upstaged and irrelevant, unheard and incapable of responding.

Some leaders began to survey the poorest of the poor, African American victims who had been unjustly shelved in urban high-rises in the name of urban renewal. Not one of them—mostly women, young mothers, or often older single women—ever mentioned anything on the Black Power agenda. The respondents shocked us by sounding so ordinary, so middle-class in their hopes and interests. Not that they were unmoved by calls to action. But their list of desires—not demands—was familiar: better protection, safe neighborhoods, better schools. Put these African Americans in a room together, and through incubation and conversation, those with ears to hear discovered problems and even some solutions.

In addition to this historical precedent, with many lessons gained from theorists of conversation, the background of this book is also a relevant reference point. Here I draw explicitly on concrete experience in the recent past. In fact, three specific conversations stand behind these pages, giving shape to the agenda and outline. Those conversations might be a model for what we hope will transpire in church and synagogue forums, parent-teacher organizations, groups of schoolteachers and university professors, and indeed for citizens in general.

These three conversations, on education and religion, were instigated by the Public Religion Project, an endeavor I directed that initiated our discussions, produced many ideas, and finally made this book possible. As described at the back of the book, the project's agenda was to "bring to light and interpret the forces of faith in a pluralist society" in a country where so many people think of religion as "a private affair." To accomplish the project's mission, we could use any strategies that would bring people together in contexts where civility would rule and yet convictions could and would be expressed. In short, the project's model was conversation, among a wide range of interests and people.

Though we didn't strictly follow the model of King's aide, you can sense how his technique influenced us on a smaller scale. At each of three conversations (one on elementary and secondary education, one on private colleges, and one on public universities), we convened approximately twenty different people around a big table, with room for others to encircle the group, listen in, and occasionally contribute. Invited were interesting combinations of people, many of whom were quite used to arguing, often with each other. The invitation list included some who held extreme positions, but in this and other instances we found that those who were most polarizing were often the most reluctant to accept our invitation, either because they mistrusted the idea of dialogue or because they have too often been merely sneered at, rather than engaged, by their opponents. No doubt those of you who want to incubate ideas and create true conversation will experience similar difficulties. Not everyone is ready to voice opinions in the presence of their foes, who are often just as ready to blast away in response. Not everyone wants to recognize the full humanity and dignity of people who differ. Many sometimes fear that their own positions might be eroded should they converse with enemies. Sometimes invitees "type" the inviters—as liberal or conservative, pro or con—and question the motivations for the invitation.

Around our table, we had advocates of home schooling and school vouchers next to individuals heavily invested in the future of public education. At the gathering to discuss church-related higher education, our conversation partners ranged from people upset that secularists had been allowed to take over to people seeking new policies to negotiate American pluralism. There were both supporters and opponents of religious studies departments in public universities and colleges. All kinds of positions on how to understand the separation of church and state were at our tables. Together these participants, in the course of conversation around the table, arrived at informal but coherent outlines of topics. We listened carefully to the concerns and ideas that arose in the discussion and took notes. They form the background for this book and, we hope, will give impetus to your own conversations about education, religion, and the common good.

This book is written with the hope that all over America, more people will be inspired not only to argue over answers to such issues but also to converse about the right questions. The following pages will bid repeatedly for your responses to this challenge. Perhaps similar issues will be taken up in conversations that you help establish. I hope so.

2

Why This Civil Conversation Is Urgent

In Chapter One, we defined *argument* as being founded on disagreement about answers to problems. *Conversation,* by contrast, we defined as being determined by questions. In conversation, we make suggestions, we are tentative, we try out this, we imagine that, we are attentive listeners, and we speak in ways that show we are open to change. No one, we noted, ever says, "I won that conversation." Instead, we arrive at the solutions together.

The conversation we begin here derives from a desire to improve the understanding of how education and religion connect and, based on that understanding, to enhance that connection in the interest of the common good. This is an urgent issue in our pluralist republic. Why? We live in a political society. Regardless of whether citizens are politically informed, interested, and active, politics is inescapable. All of us are born into a world where the political order surrounds us, in the form of taxes, government programs, national defense, and the like. Political leaders, who carefully watch polls and listen to focus groups, can substantially affect our lives by their actions. It is worth listening to them, even as they condense their messages and programs into sound bites.

In listening to those sound bites at the turn of the twenty-first century, one often hears references to "education"—as in "I will be an education governor" or "I want to be remembered by what I did for education." In polls, education may not be named as the most pressing issue. But when citizens argue about the young, about the quality of life, about skills people can acquire, they respond to appeals to improve education.

The impulse to learn and to know is undoubtedly universal. Children may not like school, but they find ways to pursue education. Those who are in colleges and universities deal not only with courses but also with what education means. Parents care. And it matters greatly where research funds go: well-spent resources may save lives, while ill-spent resources can kill. In some towns, opponents of public school bond issues have been known to bus senior citizens to the polls, assuming that they will vote against such funding measures. Their children are long past school age, so why should these seniors pay for someone else's schooling? Perhaps because they care about the whole health of society. Voters who care about themselves alone do not realize that they inhabit worlds where education matters.

I cannot stress too often that this book treats all education, elementary through postdoctoral, public and private, as of one piece. What goes on in these forms and on these levels affects the complex republic. When these agencies fail, the results affect society even more. You may not have children in parochial or private schools and may never have darkened the doorways of any of them yourself. But we hope to convince you to share our concerns with these schools, for they affect you nevertheless. They have particular gifts and challenges, and they impinge on public life—*all* of public life—in surprising ways.

Similarly, you may belong to a significant minority that puts most of its energy into private or parochial schools. We should not have to work hard to convince you to stay with our discussion of public education. You are made aware of this educational sphere through the act of paying taxes, and you know that public institutions outnumber you and can affect all of public life.

Whoever cares about this nation's future must care about education. What scholars do in laboratories, what thinkers generate, what teachers at all levels exemplify and impart, all this bears on the immediate and future life of the republic.

Religion's Place in All This

On the surface, the intersections of religion and education may not be obvious. Many people think of religion as only a private affair, something that takes place in a home or sanctuary, with little public consequence. We Americans are also taught to think of American society as a secular one in which religion does not count for much, and our educational system is organized in such a way that religious concerns often receive little attention. But if you think for a moment, you may realize that a better question is, where does religion *not* come into all this? You will not get very far into any educational issues without somehow bumping into religious themes. You can ruin town meetings and dinner parties by raising such topics as school prayer, character formation, teaching morals, the state of the younger generation, or the extremes of campus life.

Many people respond angrily when questions about schooling arise. Some are enraged by reports of disrespectful and even violent students. Who or what is responsible for this? The Supreme Court, which "took God out of the schools" in the 1960s? Secularists, who happily helped speed God's exit from education? Other parents, who have clearly neglected to instruct their children to fear and love God?

Others hear that compared to the "good old days," education's quality has slipped dramatically. Seniors may recall that they were well educated in the "four Rs"—reading, 'riting, 'rithmetic, and religion. Where, many ask, is that fourth R now?

Also angry are parents who frequent parent-teacher organizations or who storm school board meetings. They want their children to be safe in a secure educational environment, which many schools fail to provide. They want their children instructed in the tried and true basics—from phonics to *McGuffey's Reader*, for some—but instead they find schools experimenting with educational models that produce less than impressive results. Some parents want children to sing *their* Christmas carols and *their* sacred hymns in holiday programs, while others don't want any particular religious prayers or works of art imposed on an increasingly diverse body of public school children.

Anger can also be heard in the voices of immigrants, who have been told that the public schools will help integrate their children into the wider culture. Some newcomers may wish the schools could do a better job of this, while others resist such integration as representing a loss of their traditional identity. Related debates ensue over bilingual education and curricula that attempt to honor and celebrate cultural and religious diversity.

Anger wells up even more strongly when public education approaches intimate life issues. Partisans stake out territory on all sides of sex education programs. Advocates for teaching sexual abstinence tangle with those who would hand out condoms to accomplish the same goal of preventing teen pregnancy. Debates swirl around "values clarification" as a supposedly neutral way to instruct children about moral issues.

Citizens also get *really* angry about more directly religious issues. If things are too quiet in your school district, try raising some of the following questions. Should there be a constitutional amendment to permit school prayer? Should children be allowed or forced to sing religious songs at holiday programs? Can there be religious images in the classroom? Should Jesuit-based universities display crucifixes on classroom walls? Should Catholic universities bow to the Vatican's guidelines and strictures concerning the proper focus of Catholic education? Must the rights of the nonreligious be respected as much as those of religious majorities? Can schools actively sponsor prayers at high school football games? Is it an intolerable blasphemy against Native American traditions to have college cheerleaders imitate Indian dances at halftime? Must Orthodox Jews be forced to live in college dormitories where both sexes live in close proximity? Should government regulate home schooling to ensure that home-schooled children are ably equipped to become good American citizens?

Innumerable questions could be added to this list. A quick glance at the indexes of the *Chronicle of Higher Education* reveals many items that represent the uneasiness, divisions, controversies, and conflicts that divide the culture and generate religious responses. I hope that these and many other questions can help set your agenda in similar conversations.

My point, I hope, is beginning to sink in: education matters. Even where people remain indifferent, education and its intersections with religion will soon generate public controversy and debate.

Education, Culture, and Religion

Running as a thread throughout much of this debate, but revealed only after prolonged inquiry, is the realization that much of the debate is not about education itself but instead is about the culture that education produces. This gives rise to another set of questions for people conversing about religion and education: If citizens expect education to be devoted to transmitting culture, to whom should they entrust it? Is teacher education today ably equipped to train teachers for such tasks? Do teachers work in situations that allow them freedom to interpret the culture, or do they labor under many restrictions?

That set of questions relates to an assumption about education. It holds that when education in any way goes beyond mere technical training, it reaches close to the very core of the ego, the self, the "person in community." And to discuss such matters without paying attention to life's religious dimensions unfairly segregates education from the rest of cultural life. Many of the other institutions that help construct and nurture the self and community freely consider religion. Does, should, must education? Why?

To help you think about the connections among education, culture, and religion, we devote the remainder of this chapter to an exercise that calls readers and conversation participants to picture a series of concentric circles that issue from, or crowd in on, an individual.[1] The boundaries between these zones are fuzzy, and their order is arbitrary, yet they serve as signals that begin to define areas that demand responsibility and creativity.

Circle 1: The Core of One's Being

Mentally draw a stick figure of a person, perhaps yourself. Then draw a circle immediately around that figure and get ready to think about how education and religion connect in this first case. Call that first circle *the core of one's being*. That core has many names, depending on who analyzes it from what angle and for what purpose. From some angles, it has to do with the self itself. Most sane people act on the basis of this center, this core, which provides energy, motivation, and perspective.

For many, this core is one's worldview, a *Weltanschauung*, an encompassing outlook on life. And if this personal core is in every case irreducible, it is also irreplaceable. A woman can live with her spouse for decades, in almost unlimited degrees of intimacy, and yet know little about some secrets of his personality or philosophy. Similarly, through the years a man may have innumerable immediate and interpersonal encounters with his wife and still not know her worldview or be able to perceive the world through her eyes.

For adults, education is often a domain that insists on testing what one holds dear. The acts of educating the young and hoping that they will affirm the parental world usually go hand in hand.

Biblical literature refers often to the way one "trains up children" in the way they should go.

In *The Invisible Religion*, Thomas Luckmann may have been a bit extreme when he wrote that all development of this core personhood has a religious dimension. There is, Luckmann contended, no purely secular world "out there" as perceived by the individual "in here." Every human asks questions of meaning in order to transcend mere biological existence. When doing so, humans likely reach for symbols, signs historically fraught with religious meanings.[2] But one does not have to be a social psychologist of religion to observe how consistently these questions of ultimate concern and symbolization arise among individuals and in societies.

At this innermost circle, we are talking about private life, intensely private life. What does any of this have to do with the common good? One's personal beliefs have an unavoidably public dimension. As people bring different core personalities and worldviews into the public where people interact, they also bring along various understandings of education's purpose. How should education contribute to the common good? What kind of society are we trying to construct? These questions trace back to what is at stake for the individual person. Let that core of the person be threatened, and the individual, out of reason or panic, must react.

Circle 2: Personal and Social Identity

Imagine a second concentric circle moving out from the person's core worldview. Label this second sphere something like *personal and social identity*.

Personal and social identity questions have to do with close-to-the-heart urgencies. Who am I? To whom do I belong? Who belongs to me? Whom shall I trust and who shall trust me? In whom do I confide? With whom do I share stories and hopes? With whom do I share common features and experiences that help us differentiate ourselves from others? What are some ways in which I organize power or share suffering with others? What, other than the nation, reinforces my personhood and worldview?

These questions have been timeless, but they may have elicited simpler answers in less pluralist, less diverse societies. If one grew up in a territory where everyone spoke the same language, shared the same faith, inherited the same customs, and lived in isolation from others, the question of social identity would be less troubling than it is for most American citizens here and now.

Education, whether through oral transmission or formal indoctrination, is a key to this identity question. People find their identities not only by contemporary reference but also in the light of what their families have traditionally believed. And this education is almost always wedded to religion or has an underpinning of religious themes. Because religion in such circumstances has to do with the reference group, the tribe, the nation, it is by definition *public religion*, which here means that it gets tested in the interactive, public sphere. One may cherish whatever private beliefs are congenial and yet closely guard one's own integrity from cultural elders and teachers. But what is private and protected part of the time takes different shapes and assigns differing priorities, depending on what happens in the public sphere.

No wonder, then, that religion in education and religious education have become such subjects of dispute in a society made up of diverse, intersecting, and overlapping groups and faiths. Nor is there much surprise that some people in this pluralist society have thought that the best way to deal with the religious issue is to rule it out of bounds, to exclude questions of faith from education and other public spheres.

Circle 3: Sexuality

Draw a third circle around the figurative citizen and label it *sexuality*. As with identity, sexuality is an issue as old as culture itself, arising in biblical accounts of creation and their counterparts. All religions have much to say about sexuality and its expressions. From the beginning, religious leaders have tried to control or affect sexual expression through publicly issued commands, prohibitions, and encouragements. Debates over cohabitation before and apart from marriage, homosexuality, and other sexual issues usually divide religious groups, who express themselves with more intensity and less flexibility in this than in most other realms.

If anything does, sexuality would seem to belong wholly to the private sphere. Well, yes, but this private matter inevitably has public consequences. There is, for instance, debate over sex education in public schools. Sex has "gone public" in advice columns, advertisements, therapeutic and counseling centers, and the world of younger generations. Universities offer "Queer Education" or "Gendered Studies" departments and forums and invite the general public to pay attention and participate.

Religion and education come together again in this intimate zone, a "private affair," but it is today very much a part of public affairs. Hence there are endless debates about how textbooks should deal with sexuality or how sexuality is treated in higher education. Religious interests regularly express themselves on all these levels.

Circle 4: Family

Draw a fourth concentric circle and label it *family*. This circle connects with and builds on the previous three, and like them, *family* initially seems to designate something that belongs in the private sphere. Indeed, many consider the family a haven from public turmoil. The family, especially in its extended form, is a center where individuals receive and reinterpret some inherited values. The family allows, even today, for a modicum of protection against alien influences and can be a shelter. While outside influences such as mass media, schools, and friends will all be distractions, some of them creative, in the family, parents can educate the young in the most decisive ways. It is not impertinent then to ask, what business does anyone in the public realm have invading this privileged zone?

So strong have many outside influences become, and so alien do they appear to parents who cherish particular values, that some parents have taken up home schooling. Such a choice may be an expression of talented parents who enjoy circumstances that permit them to tutor their children and not send them to any formal schools. Or home schooling may be the choice of aggressively defensive parents who want to shield their children from diverse experiences and stimuli. In such settings, parents may be able to equip children with special ideas and meanings that, at least in the eyes of parents, not only do not get much public support but often are even undercut by public interests.

To show how interconnected these spheres of experience are, we can look back now and see how the family relates to the other zones and how education and religion play, or may play, a part in all. Those who cherish family life and values will argue credibly that nowhere is there more opportunity to influence a child's worldview than in the family. If religion is to be central to one's existence, the idea of having children educated where religion is systematically screened out from consideration may be troubling. If religion has to do with personal identity, it will concern family members as they ponder how one is initiated into a class or a school where identities get blurred and particular interpretations of life are treated negatively. If religion has much to do with one's sexuality and gender, what happens if a school undermines a family's religious outlook? Religion is consistently attentive to the meanings and practices that have to do with whatever gets defined as family. When it comes to interpreting family life, most citizens regard the subject as laden with religious meanings.

Circle 5: Education

Next, draw a fifth concentric circle around our citizen, the *education* circle. Since we're discussing education on every page of this book, we'll not elaborate too much here, but religion as an organizing category must be seen as relevant in this sphere. Religion's salience can be proved by raising any number of questions. Who owns the child? The parents? The state? What rights does the child have? Should tax-supported institutions of higher education sponsor religious studies departments? Should state universities have chaplains whose salary is drawn from the funds of believers and non-believers alike? These are public, often political questions, and all reflect a sense of what much of the public conceives of as religious. When someone raises such questions, there is no place to hide; it is impossible to discuss such subjects fully without making an informed address to the religious dimensions.

Circle 6: Health and Well-Being

Now draw a sixth circle and label it *health and well-being*. This includes all dimensions of medicine, health care, and the well-being of both body and spirit. No doubt the chronically or progressively ill, the differently abled, hypochondriacs, the depressed, and the health-obsessed would put this sphere closer to the core, right after and next to their own worldviews. Whatever the sequence, this zone is of vital importance, demonstrated by what proportion of national and personal wealth goes into health care and medical services.

"How are you?" A bore has been defined as someone who, when asked that question, actually answers it. But more seriously, the conventional "How are you?" is also a genuine bid issued dozens of times a day by people who interact with others. And even when it is not vocally expressed, that "how" often gets translated to an inquiry about health and well-being that reflexively invites response. I must have the answer to "How are you?" before I can relate to you. It matters greatly whether a person responds with "I'm fine" or with "I have a just-diagnosed brain tumor."

That health interests relate to education is obvious, beginning with children's hygiene and physical education classes. Education is crucial with respect to strategies that work for prevention of disease, information about dangerous medicines and projects, advice columns, or what transpires in advanced medical schools. As well, many adult retreats are devoted to holistic and alternative medicine.

Religion also has its place in matters of health and well-being. How past religious educators and leaders viewed the body—by forbidding dissection or autopsies, for example—was a public issue. The modern discipline of bioethics or medical ethics, though often focused on an individual in the privacy of an intensive care unit, also deals with questions of justice with respect to allocating resources or providing access to health care. The public has to be concerned not only with how state universities deal with health issues but also with the endeavors of a Bible college that sends graduates out to spread a particularly religious understanding of public health.

By now you probably see why we said that the sequence of these concentric circles is somewhat arbitrary—many individuals would rearrange and reprioritize them. Philosopher Ernest Gellner deals with problems of identity when he speaks of "modular man," the person who puts himself together in changing ways, but always in light of many arrangements and stimuli.[3] Just as parts of a modular sofa or bookcase may be broken apart into segments, allowing for many options for rearranging a room, so the self can acquire many different identities and rearrange them in various creative ways. The exact location or sequence of the circles you've drawn matters less than understanding that all of them are very close to the person. Draw as many other spheres of perception and action as you like. What we have already done, we hope, is convinced the skeptic in you that education is often inevitably charged with religious meanings. And we hope to have persuaded you that even the private expressions of religion and education "go public" more than occasionally and often in unforeseen ways.

Now that we've explored ways in which education relates to different stages of life in different ways, we'll take these up in successive chapters. With understandings of education, religion, and the common good in mind, it's time to listen in on and participate in a conversation. Let the conversation begin!

3

A Historical Map
of the Present Situation

We can assume that in any polity that encourages homogeneity rather than celebrates diversity, teachers would have an easier time deciding what to teach. And in the early days of the republic, that was exactly the situation in America: only the majority Protestant faith was officially privileged.

But the American circumstance was historically distinctive. Ordinarily, religious uniformity was born of the union of religion and regime. Behind this form of governance usually stood the belief that one God rules both state and society. In such a worldview, God may rule by deputizing or making vicars out of various earthbound leaders, and the consequent forms of government acquire names such as "theocracy," "hierocracy," or "clerocracy." In all such contexts, the ruler determines the boundaries within which the philosophy and content of education emerge. The only controversy to follow in such situations concerns whether a teacher follows or departs from the "party line" or whether an independently thinking student, risking punishment, speaks up.

In ancient Israel, God set divine commands forth clearly. "Train up the child in the way he should go" was a command not necessarily followed by everyone, but the demand simplified life by describing only one way to follow. There were no courses in positive interfaith relations or comparative religion to provide equal time for Canaanite and Egyptian religions alongside the Yahwistic faith.

In the long span of Christian history since the fourth century, educating the young—such as it occurred in the court or among the peasantry—could continue to follow clear, singular norms. One official church emerged and produced a context called Christendom, in which Christianity's domain was the entire culture. Of course, Christians regularly improvised their own popular religions, often in contradiction to the officially approved faith. The historical record shows that common people in particular dealt with magic, astrology, omens, and relics alongside the orthodox transcendent God. Yet even then, those interests were filtered and focused by the light of particular faith in Jesus. Whenever the young were catechized, however infrequently, it was clear what should be taught and counseled. The elder and established generation passed on to the young a single world, word, and truth, drawing or coercing a new generation into assent.

The sixteenth-century Renaissance, the eighteenth-century Enlightenment, the ages of world exploration, and the rise of modern science in the West all set the stage for a new drama. The British Revolution of 1688, the American Revolution of 1776, and the French Revolution of 1789 all helped usher in changes in the once unquestioned political model. Whereas the British and French came more slowly to the idea, the United States eventually resituated religion in the First Amendment to the Constitution in 1789. Americans officially severed the traditional bond between church and state.

Near the end of the eighteenth century, religious freedom gradually increased, and the educated developed a new awareness of how others believed and worshiped, thanks to the reports of explorers, settlers, and colonists and as a result of curiosities and criticisms stemming from the Enlightenment. In the early nineteenth century, the citizens of the new United States created what some have called a "second establishment" in place of the old and abolished legal one. This version simply privileged the religion of the majority, which was a kind of generalized Protestantism that much later came to be called "mainstream" or "mainline." This majoritarian faith mingled with a genial pattern of democratic "secular" thought associated with the Enlightenment, and that fusion inspired and predominated in nineteenth-century American schoolbooks.

Initially, public schools reflected the outlook and ethos of the nation's founders. They adhered to and propagated a philosophy that historian Crane Brinton called "a new religion," "Enlightenment with a 'Big E.'"[1] This Enlightenment faith—some called it deism, but that is too precise a term for a very vague faith—was dedicated to morality. Though many believers in outsider faiths contended that religion should be mainly about divine revelation or specifics like grace, this Enlightenment religion was designed to be generic, universal. Founders like Washington, Adams, Jefferson, and Madison were tolerant with respect to religious belief. They helped construct a constitutional system that guaranteed religious liberty for the most recalcitrant and idiosyncratic faiths. But in private correspondence, these founders often revealed their impatience with expressions of faith that departed significantly from their own norms. Thus Thomas Jefferson derided John Calvin's Trinity as being more about mathematics than about religion. With respect to communal faith, Jefferson and Thomas Paine liked to say that their own minds were their temples; if they had to go to heaven with a group, they would not go.[2]

One of the great breaches in this program—one that is still with us today—had to do with whether or not there was a need for special revelation in scripture. Jeffersonians and people like Benjamin Franklin were devoted to what they called Nature's God, to capitalized concepts such as Reason and Natural Law. This God and this Law were accessible through Reason, so one did not need a book that claimed special revelation. While they might have respected it, the Bible was not a revelation necessary for salvation above and governance below. Some people—like Jefferson—were capable of cutting the miraculous and the supernatural out of the Gospels, the better to see Jesus as teacher and moral exemplar, not divine Messiah. Unlike the revivalists, they would prosper not through emotional appeals but through reason.

As the founding generation passed, the Enlightenment view was overtaken by these revivalists and others who stressed emotion, revelation, and salvation. But the founders' influence was felt in the establishment of common and public schools at midcentury, and it lives on in the various "religions of democracy" that educators such as John Dewey have since celebrated.

In his 1945 work *The New Education and Religion*, J. Paul Williams offered the most extreme effort to generate a form of public education that was democratic rather than religiously particular. In this book and successive editions of his later book, *What Americans Believe and How They Worship*, Williams argued that it was not enough for individual religions to promote private, ceremonial, and aesthetic values. For the common good there had to be a Religion of Democracy. "Metaphysical sanctions" and "ceremonial reinforcements" would support this endeavor to teach this democratic religion as society's way of life.[3]

But the hold of the common faith on the American people began to loosen as those people became increasingly more religiously diverse. Catholics and immigrants from places other than northwestern Europe had been arriving in sufficient numbers to challenge the monopoly of the old educational establishment. The presence of new peoples challenged everything that had previously been privileged, including once unquestioned educational assumptions.

After the end of World War II, in the middle of the twentieth century, many Americans dreamed of a nation where a three-faith model would replace the old Protestant one. Sociologist and theologian Will Herberg outlined what was then going on in his famed book, *Protestant-Catholic-Jew*. Herberg hypothesized that Americans were finding their postwar identities through those three large and general faith communities. Yet they all together amounted to a "civic faith."[4] A dozen years later, sociologist Robert N. Bellah called this generalized American faith "civil religion,"[5] and that name stuck.

Most Americans live genially with the fabric of this more general faith. In their eyes, it has produced good effects, and they cannot believe that it must contend with biblical faith or church religion. After all, the founders were themselves church members and generally spoke well of religious institutions. Today, say many Americans, their neighbors down the block may be Jews or Christians of various sorts and they seem to be coexisting just fine with this generalized religion. Why should anyone worry?

By the time Bellah wrote his article in 1967, the synthetic civil faith was beginning to break apart. The national and patriotic dimensions of civil religion did not stand up to assaults from critics of the Vietnam War. Feminists noted just how patriarchal the old religiomoral synthesis had been, fashioned as it was by assertive men. African American Protestants, Hispanic Catholics, and Native Americans did not find *their* religious sensibilities represented in this civil religion either. In this era, pluralism was morphing into multiculturalism. Various groups expressed their separate identities, and they opposed the comprehensive and general civic faith or civil religion.

There are other criticisms of this common-faith model. For example, some evangelicals who start their own schools but would like to return to or even recapture the public schools have their own spin on this history. They charge that a conspiracy of "secular humanist" elites have commandeered the schools. They argue that these humanists have corrupted the religion of the founders. To make this argument persuasive, they often try to make the founders sound more distinctively evangelical, or at least more broadly Christian, than some of these adherents of the "Big E" religion wanted to be.

The twentieth-century passage from a one-faith to a three-faith to a multifaith model can be traced in several ways. For example, a reference work such as *The Readers' Guide to Periodical Literature* displays almost no citations for the present-day concept of "pluralism" during the first half of the twentieth century. (Only a few allusions to philosophical pluralism, à la William James, make it into the record.) But during the second half of the twentieth century, pluralism became the new and challenging context for school classrooms. Whatever else the shift to pluralism and later multiculturalism meant, no longer would Protestantism and its culture be privileged. No longer would the kind of biblical witness of Protestant Christianity be given legal support. And especially after great waves of immigrants arrived around the start of the century, after World War II, and again after changes in immigration laws in 1965, no longer could teachers assume that they could freely and safely offer a Christian interpretation of reality to their students.

To complicate matters further for education, religious pluralism was increasingly acknowledged on a federal and legal level. From the beginning of the United States in 1789 until the 1940s, few Supreme Court decisions touched on matters of church and state or, more specifically, religion and education. But in the 1940s, the Court began to apply the Bill of Rights (including its First Amendment guidelines on religion and government) to the states. Subsequently, the Court began to restructure the relationship between religion and public education.

In a 1948 case, *McCollum v. Board of Education*, the Supreme Court disallowed released-time programs that allowed schoolchildren to receive religious instruction during the normal school day. In its majority opinion, the Court said that as a symbol of democracy, the public schools should be kept free from religious influences. "If nowhere else," one justice wrote, "in the relation between Church and State, 'good fences make good neighbors.'" Fourteen years later, in 1962, the Supreme Court disallowed prayer in public schools in *Engel v. Vitale*, and a year after that, in *Abington School District v. Schempp*, the Court also ruled unconstitutional the practice of Bible-reading in public schools.

What eventually emerged came to be called, around the middle of the twentieth century, religious pluralism. The argument that this pluralism must be recognized, realized, and indeed celebrated colors much of the present debate on our subject. In the middle of the twentieth century, a new chapter had begun, and the story of this tension between the one and the many, religiously speaking, is not over yet.

4

Religion and Education
The Pitfalls of Engaging a Complex Issue

The complicated historical dimensions of religion and education in America color the present scene in a variety of ways.
Though a great many factors make this issue a difficult one to
engage, tackling the subject is ultimately not only worthwhile but
in fact necessary.

Relevant Differences Between
Higher and Lower Education

One key complication, especially in a book calling for treating the
subject comprehensively, is that there are indeed real and important differences between higher and lower education. First of all,
one obvious difference between the two levels of education has to
do with the critical faculties of the audience. College instructors
can assume (or at least hope for) a modicum of critical judgment on
the part of students, who can take what they study and what they
hear in a variety of ways: tentatively, quizzically, or antagonistically.
The same is certainly not true of younger audiences. Students in
their early teens have not yet developed the critical acumen they
will rely on only a few years later. While college students can tell
the difference between imparting information and proselytizing,
individuals at earlier education levels may not be able to do so. In

elementary schools especially, where students often have a single teacher for most subjects, children may be more gullible, more easily influenced and manipulated, more exploitable.

Another key difference between these two levels of education has to do with the role of parents. In elementary and high schools, parents and other adults can still do some filtering of information, allowing them to whittle complex realities down to understandable data. With the adult buffers around them, children of elementary and even high school age are less likely to be hurt by ignorance about religion's role in the wider world. On the college level, there are many reasons to argue for including religion in the curriculum. Indeed, it is not only valuable but urgent for adults to be informed about religion. Knowledge of religious matrices and motivations can help students negotiate their way in a global economy. Such knowledge can even be lifesaving, enabling one to recognize the real and merely apparent dangers among fanatical religious groups. University graduates will soon be neighbors to strangers and will be better citizens for understanding those strangers and their worldviews. On public occasions when civil inoffensiveness is appropriate, knowledge of religions can ably assist. All of these reasons are less urgent at the grade school level.

Even in grade school, however, we know and tell lighthearted stories about the social and personal costs of religious ignorance. Johnny, a Protestant boy who always plays with Catholic neighbors, comes home with a black eye. "What happened?" his parents demand. "Well," Johnny explains, "I was making wisecracks over at the Kellys, and Kevin Kelly got angry and socked me in the eye." Parent: "What were you wisecracking about?" Johnny: "Oh, about the pope." Parent: "But Johnny, surely you knew that the Kellys were Catholic!" "Of course I did," said Johnny. "I just didn't know the pope was." Ignorance only gets costlier as children grow older.

In spite of these differences, we maintain that it still makes sense to see all of education from preschool to postgraduate on a single continuum, as we are doing here. Focusing on one education level can help illuminate other parts of the sequence, as we hope the rest of the book will demonstrate.

Illegitimate Fears: Establishment, Relativism, and Indifference

Bringing religion into the public school curriculum is not without dangers, and we would do well to be aware of them. Some parents may fear that their children, introduced to various religious faiths, may soon slide into a debilitating relativism where all spiritual options are equal.

Others will resent the introduction of religion because they would like to control which rites and ceremonies, which classroom topics, should be included or excluded. Some parents may want only one religion, their own, presented to their children as a legitimate worldview. After all, public schools may end up teaching about certain subjects that some parents find objectionable, which may weaken a faith's hold on young minds. Making room for religion in the classroom, in the wrong hands, can end up making room for only one religion to the exclusion of others.

Clearly, studying religion must be accomplished in ways that avoid running afoul of the Constitution's prohibition against establishing religion. Educators and parents must be attentive to methods that do not violate Jefferson's separation of church and state or cross Madison's line of distinction between religious and civil authorities. But teaching religion can be faithful to the founders' intentions. They were careful that the government not establish a religion or religions so as not to privilege one religion over another or religion over nonreligion and also so that religion would *not* be a liability for citizens who enter the public arena.

Church-state separation traditions give good reasons for citizens to be careful about introducing or expanding subjects like religion in tax-supported public institutions. Religion is bad stuff from the word *go*, say some, and the more we can leave it out of the classroom and curriculum, the better off we will be. Put it on the shelf with astrology and other subjects that millions care about but that are not appropriate for serious pedagogy.

Introducing religion on curricular terms, say others, only opens the way for proselytizing and witnessing groups to get a foot in the door and to introduce elements of competition to the school scene. The aggressive groups, these critics note, are best poised to take part in religious discussion, and they will exploit the opportunity. Meanwhile more tolerant, ecumenically minded groups will be pushed into the background, and their children will be subjected to pesky and assertive witnesses.

Shouldn't the religiously minded stop clamoring for more attention to religious concerns and be a bit more generous about the republic? This scene is already overrun by competing interest groups: parochial schools, voucher advocates, released-time proponents, textbook revisers, critics of any governmental involvement in education—just to name a few. Why encourage more disruption in a locale that is already being overrun by competing forces? Why beckon the activities of these interest groups, who don't always care that much about the common good? Controversies in society can and should be pursued on the basis of "secular rationality," argue some, and introducing approaches congenial to religion will only complicate the proper, "reasonable" approach to everything.

Criticisms come from all sides. Some religious people will have trouble dealing with religion as a subject one can teach the young "about." When teachers teach "about" religion, faith may either get reduced to something so bland that it leads to a misreading of religion or become something so volatile that it will disrupt school and community life. And anyway, we should not expect the school to do everything. Moral education, to which religion in part relates, is accidental, incidental, and diffuse in schools. Putting it on the agenda weighs a school down. We already ask the schools to be babysitters, entertainers, and recreation leaders. Why make them do more? What, after all, are families and houses of worship for?

Moreover, the curriculum is already overcrowded, the textbooks are too long, and homework is too burdensome. You just can't keep piling on more. Colleges and universities have enough trouble handling the philosophical questions sparked by religion. How and why burden junior and senior high schools with such subjects and problems?

Another related difficulty is that religion deals so much with texts. How can education relate the different ways the academy and religious communities approach such texts? Even high school sophomores would necessarily be thrust into the rudiments of literary and historical criticism of ancient scriptures, and there'd be hell to pay when they report back home on how this does not square with what they've previously been taught.

In the end, many observers ask, won't you be contributing to relativism among children? In public schools, teachers and texts would have to give a basically positive spin to most features of most religions. Won't students then conclude that all religions are nice, that they are all about the same business? Won't they be led to think that it does not and will not make any difference what religious choices people make or what traditions and truth-claims they have inherited?

Teacher Training

Perhaps one of the most compelling difficulties is the issue of teacher training. Worriers assert that there are not and will never be enough teachers who can competently teach about religion or even guide discussion of religion when the subject comes up on its own. Scholars who devote decades to this study tend to be specialists who are wary of treating something beyond their competence.

The sixteen-volume *Encyclopedia of Religion* next to shelves full of registers, atlases, dictionaries, and directories suggests that a bewildering variety of religions exist, and hundreds, even thousands of these are active in the United States. How can someone be prepared to deal with the varieties that are likely to come up even in one locale, one classroom?

How, especially, can there be preparation if education departments, where teacher training goes on, have no place for the appraisal of religion? If religion by "natural inclusion" comes up mainly in social scientific courses, should everyone in teacher training have to learn enough about religion to be able to negotiate its elements in a junior high classroom? If nothing happens on the teacher training level, religion would get treated in amateur fashion, while other social scientific topics would continue to reflect professionalism.

If nothing happens at all in teacher training, the teacher who must deal, who gets to deal, with this subject would likely be tempted to fall back on impressions gained from moving about in a particular culture. Or perhaps worse, the teacher might rely on vestiges of religion picked up in Sabbath or Sunday schools. The problem with that is that such learning, dispensed originally to infant, young child, or preadolescent, will seem simplistic when set alongside subjects studied in college.

So we have a problem. Although it is too soon for a complete program of approaches to the topic of religion in the schools, school districts can and should begin now with very modest and minimal expectations. As textbook writers act on the principle of "natural inclusion," which some have begun to do, teachers will have better materials to rely on and more durable resources. There are also now excellent video and audio materials, prepared by experts who are sensitive to the delicacy of the subject. Both trust and curiosity will grow as more and more classrooms effectively pursue teaching about religion and its place in society.

Meanwhile, after the "very modest and minimal expectations" stage in elementary and high school has passed, those who wish can pursue the subject on the college and university level, where participants can move far beyond the notion of natural inclusion. Then religion can be isolated and treated on its own terms.

Making religion part of public school curricula will likely require some training and retraining of teachers. Of course, we are not talking about doctorate-level critical approaches but simpler ones intended to reach the minds of children aged six to eighteen. Educating the educators should help teachers recognize and understand spiritual nuances, religious commitments, and practices with the same competence required of them in other disciplines.

Maybe the best one can expect—and this is a great deal—is that teachers be well-rounded, always alert citizens who are good listeners and speakers who read situations well. For the rest, "handle with care" is not a bad reminder to put on any ventures by people who have the young entrusted to them.

All of these arguments and claims must be acknowledged. Indeed, they should form part of the agenda for discussion. Nevertheless, in spite of these difficulties, we still maintain that conversation about religion, education, and the common good is both necessary and worthwhile.

Perhaps for many this will seem utopian—or dystopian, for those who oppose any form of religion in schools. Yet when handled with care, religion can be properly included in public schools, and in fact it is being included with increasing success in hundreds of schools today.

The Explosion of Knowledge

Public education also must contend with the ramifications of new technologies. As technical learning manifestly and increasingly takes over from humanistic and social scientific inquiry, even the most beneficent educators may have trouble finding room for religion in the curriculum. There are too many other important ways to allocate classroom time, especially when teachers are charged with preparing students for life in an increasingly technology-driven world. And in communities where religion stirs controversy, whether inside or outside the school walls, avoiding religion becomes an easy and obvious plan of action.

The growth of knowledge has affected the public school classroom in various ways. For example, many conservative Protestants urge the teaching of creationism, whereas most Protestants, Catholics, and Jews find such teachings unsound. Similarly, religious people disagree over sex education policies precisely because they have different interpretations of authoritative moral codes. What is the appropriate alternative when worldviews interpret certain subjects differently? Is the only alternative a dispassionate, supposedly objective, disinterested approach to morals and worldviews? Not really, because it is impossible to refuse any option at all. As conservative religionists point out, *not* having an interpretation is in itself an interpretation. Everyone, even the supposedly neutral, speaks from a particular point of view.

General Confusion

Meanwhile, in the public schools, leaders have had to make many adjustments to cultural and legal changes. Sometimes actions were quite conscious and universal, while at other times their moves were more or less impromptu. One example concerned the propriety and legality of having choirs sing religious songs in holiday programs. Similarly, teachers and administrators often remained uncertain and confused about what exactly could be said about religion in the classroom. America had grown religiously diverse enough that a teacher could no longer assume a consensus about values and faith on the part of students or, especially, their parents.

How to teach "about" religion without implying judgments of truth or error? Sometimes professionals opted to change the subject entirely.

Religion as a specific truth about life, taught in such a pluralist context, would have to be so thinned out that it would lose the complexity and intensity of faith lived in believing communities. If the public school offers a cafeteria line of religious options and regards each option equally, children may be less likely to pursue faith with integrity in their own families and social groups. While teaching about religions in a neutral way may help check some of the passions that particularist faith communities often produce, it is just as possible that sympathetic encounters with other faiths may loosen the hold of one's own tradition.

Some writers have observed that in the nineteenth century, Americans had an easier time criticizing faraway Buddhists while asserting the superiority of Christian truth. Why? Back then, missionaries wrote home about the "bad Buddhists" and "bad Buddhism" in a distant land. But what does one do when one's own Christian seventh grader sits next to a nice young Buddhist classmate? The passion for conversion may naturally be lessened.

Pluralism has also brought into the classroom a host of other complicating elements that spark inquiry and debate. For example, an obvious issue is religious dress. Canadians have debated about when and under what circumstances Sikh university students could wear their ceremonial knives, as religiously mandated in some interpretations. In a school with a universal dress code, what about Muslim girls who must be veiled? What about schoolchildren who, because of their religious upbringing, refuse to wear the "revealing" clothes required in physical education class? Won't any exceptions to such rules begin to break down school discipline?

Many wonder why the interests of the majority seem to have disappeared. Some critics of Supreme Court decisions like to claim that there is more religious freedom in post-Soviet Russia than there is in American public schools. Not yet ready to wrestle with the public consequences of thoroughgoing pluralism, the American majority had its sensibilities violated by these decisions. Many had not thought through the implications of what government-sponsored or -authorized devotions, Bible reading, and prayer might mean in schools where many children no longer share in this part of the Christian tradition.

Should not godly America change this situation? After all, 85 percent of American people identify with the biblical faiths of Judaism and Christianity. Even with the recent growth of other faiths such as Islam and Buddhism, in twenty years the majority percentage will drop only about 2 points. Why should the majority have its voice muffled, its preferences suppressed, by religious minorities? Why not simply allot proportional time to all faiths in public schools so that everyone has space appropriate to their numbers? Somehow, it often sounds as if smart and respectful people could work all this out, were it not for the unwelcome intrusions of a few militant secularists and groups like the American Civil Liberties Union.

More credible if less passionate conflicts arise when some complain that public schools today too often deny the religious richness of America's cultural heritage. Why should "Rudolph the Red-Nosed Reindeer" come to represent the holiday season when there is a centuries-old musical tradition in Christianity, the majority American faith? Especially when public schools so carefully honor *other* religious traditions and holidays in the name of multiculturalism, why not draw on Christianity when celebrating certain occasions?

We call this complaint more credible because there are differences between worship and performance. In the concert hall, people of other faiths sing Christian choral music that derives from central themes of the biblical plot. Clearly, Jews are not worshiping when they sing or hear or raise funds for the performance of choral works by Johann Sebastian Bach. Many of his compositions have texts that are distinctively Christian and even alien and alienating to Jews. This is not to suggest that Christians are never insensitive or that Jews should not sometimes stand back when some New Testament lines create problems for them. Instead, this is to highlight the unavoidably religious dimensions of much American cultural expression.

Serious and thoughtful people need to do more homework on how best to understand and teach the differences between sacred meanings in performance and in worship. If we cannot find ways to improve in this area, we risk culturally impoverishing our children in a way that is more damaging than mere exposure to other faiths. It underestimates their potential to say that high schoolers cannot come to understand the difference in these issues. Take students to an art museum and let them learn to appreciate Buddhist art, under the guidance of a teacher or a docent who may be Buddhist, and they will be richer for it. Exposing students to Buddhist art will not make them Buddhist, but it will make them more culturally literate.

The Moral Dimension

The last and probably most important complicating factor in debates about religion and education is that of *morals*. The nation's founders and creators of common schools were uncommonly concerned with morals and civic virtue. Having just "killed the king" in the War of Independence, they were fashioning a constitutional republic under the rule of law. To succeed, the people could not be made to behave simply for fear of punishment, for there would never be enough police to ensure compliance. The founders believed that the new republic depended on a virtuous citizenry. People had to be responsible, and to be so, they had to be moral.

Echoes of this connection between morality and citizenship can be heard in more recent American cultural disputes. Many conflicts take place against the backdrop of widespread concern over perceived moral decline. For many people, public education is the place to inculcate morality, sharpen moral sensibilities, and undergird ethical action. This assumption informs the public division over the performance and potential of public education, and citizens also divide over which available instruments should be used to teach morals and civic virtue.

Like debates over devotion, these moral disputes have a long history in American life. Citizens sometimes appeal to the nation's founders as defenders of religion-friendly philosophies. However, while the Reason and Nature they appealed to sometimes suggested an integral connection to God, this was a God accessible to all people, not just those who claimed particular revelations or scriptures. A republic could not be built on the basis of particular and conflicting revelations; instead, a more general, common-denominator religion would suffice.

Others point to George Washington's famous Farewell Address or the Northwest Ordinance of 1785 to argue that the founders considered morality and religion indispensable to the republic's health. Washington called morality and religion the "twin pillars" of the republic. The Northwest Ordinance provided for morality and religion as part of schooling, including the universities that would soon dot the landscape. There are other examples and occasions of the nation's political and educational leaders appealing to specifically Christian or Protestant affirmations, which supports the historical argument that public education was not to be value- or religion-free.

This common view was easier to achieve in the days of a more homogeneous society; in our time, citizens of all sorts agree that it has become more and more difficult to teach a uniform morality. Why? There are just too many competing worldviews. Each voice has something to say about the common good, the true, the beautiful, and these voices often contradict each other. How can schools negotiate this metaphysical and moral pluralism without implying the inferiority or superiority of certain worldviews?

One solution to pluralism is to place all contending beliefs on equal footing, but many observers claim that this relativism creates a bigger problem than it solves. We can define relativism as having one foot on a banana peel, morally speaking—and the other foot also on a banana peel. Everything becomes slippery. With morality as a matter of personal preference, there is nothing secure to hold on to, and no one can gain a sure moral footing. "You have your values and I have mine," people say. "Who am I to judge your morals, and who are you to judge mine?" Some college teachers report that when trying to place boundaries around this moral relativism, they might introduce an extreme example: if morality is a matter of mere preference, with no value system better than another, then what about judging the values of Adolf Hitler? And the shocking answer comes, not always cynically: Well, what about his values?

If all standards for judging right from wrong are relative, moral claims seem to be rooted only in feeling, experience, or personal preference. Gone from the moral scene, say critics, is any sense of God as Absolute Truth. Only with God anchoring morality can there be an objective standard, they argue. Only then can people know *exactly* what is right or wrong.

Only by objectively knowing right from wrong can adults instruct children in the moral life. Here Aristotle's influence shows: people do not become moral just by discussing the good or the ethical; they become so by practice. People must find appropriate models and pattern themselves after those models. They must put into practice the pursuit of "the good" until it becomes a habit. And if the habit is rooted in belief in God, then you can at least have a good argument about how all this works out in society. Throw the divine anchor overboard, and people are left to drift on the open waters of relativism.

People legitimately concerned about the moral situation can add in one more dimension to the discussion: government and the courts are far too responsive to pluralism and diversity, especially the religious variety. Most Americans respond to the Judeo-Christian tradition, which means that they derive morality from the same sources. Most believe that somehow God speaks to us through the Ten Commandments and that indeed God may have literally provided the commandments on stone tablets to Moses on Mount Sinai long ago. So why have the courts disallowed the display of the Decalogue in public school classrooms? Not only do most Americans believe in the importance of these moral guidelines, but these laws put forth moral principles on which almost everyone agrees. Hence there is a majoritarian argument embedded within the issue of morals.

The more ecumenically minded may suggest lifting parallel teachings from other major religions and then teaching those distilled values in a combined form. For example, many leaders of interfaith groups argue that something like the Golden Rule belongs not just to Christianity but to almost every religious tradition. Treat others as you would like to be treated, and do not treat others as you would not like to be treated. It sounds very simple and commonsensical, and of course this principle can be taught as common sense or good advice. But what one cannot do is ask children to obey the Golden Rule because God wants them to do so. Yet dropping the transcendent reference, for many people, means dropping the main reason for following such a principle. The Ten Commandments become watered down into the Ten Suggestions—or less. So what begins as a well-intentioned debate over morals in education soon turns into a theological debate that divides school boards, teachers' groups, and parent-teacher associations.

Short of abandoning moral education completely, others have tried to negotiate ethical pluralism by promoting "values clarification." It certainly sounds like a good idea: teachers and students bring their own value systems, and in the classroom they clarify them, to see what might or might not motivate valuable action. But critics swoop in at once: students not only bring to school competing value systems, which leads to confusion, but they might also bring in ideas and behaviors that most of polite society finds unacceptable. No matter how antisocial, fanatical, or dogmatic, in this system those values cannot be discouraged, only "clarified." Won't the child who has undergone values clarification not only be more confused but even less likely to act morally?

Through all these debates and behind all these questions are strong religious interests. While you can have interesting public debates about educational philosophy and moral development, people who pursue philosophical options are not as well organized into competing camps as religious groups are. The religious landscape has many polarities: fundamentalist and liberal in Protestantism, Orthodox and Reform in Judaism, conservative and liberal in Catholicism. It is no wonder that school boards and textbook authors tread cautiously when dealing with moral education. But they often fail to realize that treading cautiously is its own kind of religious or metaphysical commitment. To many religious adherents, it looks as though a competing worldview—such as "secular humanism"—has become the established or privileged religion by default, while the regular voices of the "ordinarily" religious are shut out.

What is clearly needed is more awareness of what motivates the courts and more public discussion about the wisdom or folly of their actions. Many options have been foreclosed already. Arguing for "equal time," no matter how reasonable and practical it sounds, does not seem to offer a clear way to a solution. Present both evolution and creationism and let the students decide? Scientists will contend that the language of their discipline has a different intent than religious critics suggest, while many religious people will resist having the language and claims of their faith converted into something that sounds scientific. Better alternatives must be sought, and conversations can help us reason toward them.

Morals and Education: A Case Study

To highlight the difficulties and possibilities in recent alternatives, let's pay attention for a moment to *The Moral Life of Schools*, a book by Philip W. Jackson, Robert E. Boostrom, and David T. Hansen.[1] Scanning the index indicates something of the authors' approach to our subject. There is one reference to "rituals and ceremonies," but these are not of a religious character. Words such as *religion*, *faith*, *spirituality*, *Judaism*, and *Christianity* do not occur at all.

To suggest how extensive and complex the whole moral issue is, we will mention the index references that begin with the adjective *moral*, as in *moral agents: ambiguity, climate, code, commentary, complexity, consequences, considerations, dimensions, education, enterprise, environment, influence, instruction, intentions, lessons, messages, models, overtones, perspective, point of view, potency, principles, questions, sensibilities, significance, upbringing,* and *well-being.*

The point of this is not to cause your eyes to glaze over. We picture this reference list as a good agenda for people who want to advance the conversation about religion and public education. Can you picture a Southern Baptist pastor who would yield "moral agency" to a Unitarian teacher? That Unitarian, the Baptist pastor has heard, implies that all religions are more or less the same in advocating goodness. Picture a Catholic who thinks that a person can create a "moral climate" for a child's full education without resorting to any of the "rituals and ceremonies" involved in the Mass or other Catholic devotions. Can you picture a Lutheran parochial school advocate who might agree that a "moral code" can be successfully followed without referring to the Ten Commandments, the Sermon on the Mount, or even Martin Luther's *Small*

Catechism? Where, after all, will the valid moral codes come from? Who should make "moral commentary"? asks the Jew who fears that if religion enters the classroom, pious Christians will take over. Try finding a fundamentalist who believes that "moral judgments" on issues such as abortion or euthanasia can make sense without referring to God.

Looking over this confusing field, some citizens will pine for the days when society could simply "coast." As late as the 1950s, perhaps, churches, synagogues, families, and associations could all carry the weight of moral discourse. There was little need, in this romantic picture, to debate the divine foundations of moral principles. But today, in this view, society has fragmented and disintegrated to such an alarming extent that there must be new strategies, and the schools must be ready to advance them. Can one coast any longer?

After extensively studying eighteen schools, Jackson, Boostrom, and Hansen concluded: "Although it was the most obvious thing to look for, formal moral instruction as a recurrent and identifiable piece of the curriculum was close to absent in the classrooms we visited. The clear exceptions were in the two Roman Catholic schools," where twenty minutes was set aside each day for religious instruction. In the Catholic high school they studied, religion was a required course for everyone, but the authors "encountered nothing remotely similar in any of the other schools."[2]

The authors also found something to reassure people who fear that competitive moral ideologies will confuse or that values clarification will confound: "There were no courses in civics of ethics, 'values clarification' sessions, Kohlbergian discussion groups, or any other form of moral instruction as a separate curricular entity in either of the other two high schools." The Catholic schools clearly connected religion and morality, and informally, of course, there were many moral overtones in many school situations. Students, the scholars noticed, were encouraged to give voice to their deepest commitments. But they said "it was seldom evident that the teacher was trying to teach a moral lesson per se."[3]

As for those "rituals and ceremonies" favored by religious people, some school occasions skirt the edges of being explicitly religious. Pep rallies, graduations, and assemblies might include the Lord's Prayer or the Pledge of Allegiance, as might ceremonies honoring a recently deceased public official or hero. The events were designed to engender "feelings of pride, loyalty, inspiration, reverence, piety, sorrow, prudence, thankfulness, and dedication."[4] Those who favor developing those attitudes are smiling, while those frown who think that deeply held morals and truths must be rooted in specific religious communities, texts, traditions, or mores. So even when schools try to do their best to avoid conflict, the culture wars begin again.

At the end of their book on the moral life of schools, Jackson, Boostrom, and Hansen promote further inquiry. Their appendix "Where Might One Go from Here?" offers an extensive, quite balanced, even excellent list of suggestions for further reading.[5] The section headed "Perspectives on the Moral," for example, alludes to moral discourse that goes back "at least as far as the Greeks." Following this are book recommendations all the way back to Plato and Aristotle and on down to modern worriers about virtue.

The religion sleuth with the right magnifying glass will realize that some of the recommended books include incidental or nostalgic commentary on religion. But only one title, Basil Mitchell's *Morality, Religious and Secular*, brings up the subject in a formal way.[6] The rest focus on philosophies and approaches such as pragmatism, idealism, or "moral development" psychological theory. The extent of what is available ought to cheer anyone who welcomes attention to virtue and morality, but it will not satisfy those who have any kind of religious interest.

Under "General References," the not-unfriendly-to-religion authors mention as appropriate "most canonical religious texts, centrally, of course, the Bible, the Koran, and the Torah." But instantly they change the subject back to philosophy and the teacher's vocation after that reference.

How people regard all of this depends on the degree to which they are content with or even inspired by "general reference" discourse on morality in a pluralist society. Jackson, Boostrom, and Hansen recognize that this is the case. They are not writing for specific confessional communities but for general publics. They cannot focus on the specific and particular approaches and contributions of Mormons or Adventists, Mennonites or Reform Jews, Muslims or Methodists, all of whom care greatly about moral development through schooling.

If "public religion" means the public dimensions of the separate religions, no one group will ever be fully satisfied. However, if "public religion" refers to something else, we can profitably discuss it. Benjamin Franklin, when he coined the term *publick religion* in 1749, referred to the overarching sets of meanings—many of them sacred—that citizens can still find in *The Moral Life of Schools* and its bibliographies.

Given the multiple complexities just discussed, schools have clearly been one of the main arenas for culture wars. But let us not forget that courts of all levels have been heavily involved in deciding issues of education and religion, and their decisions have often provided the occasions for public debate and anger. The courts have had to determine the constitutionality of teacher-directed school prayer, devotions, Bible reading, voluntary student-led prayer, and religious extracurricular groups. The courts have ruled on controversies concerning Jehovah's Witnesses and the Pledge of Allegiance and whether or not Amish children should be forced to attend high school.

Given the controversial nature of most of these cases, few rulings satisfied large portions of the American population. In every poll since the early 1960s, most Americans have indicated that they disagree with the Supreme Court's decisions to disallow official prayer and Bible reading in public schools. Indeed, a majority of Americans favor a constitutional amendment to legalize prayer in school. Just as firmly, on the other side, advocates have dug in and defended the Court's rulings, and many remain vigilant lest those prohibitions be violated.

The difficulties are many, but we hope this chapter hasn't discouraged you from engaging religion, education, and the common good. Whoever wants to take on these issues would do well to be aware of these sentiments, traditions, and customs that surround all sides and all positions on this scene. Understanding the hurdles ahead can prove to be valuable for generating productive, constructive conversation.

5

Why Religion Belongs in Publicly Funded Primary and Secondary Education

You do not have to be a careful reader to see that we are treating this subject gingerly. Any school districts that experiment will soon find that the ridge on which they are operating is narrow or their perch is precarious—but the view is stunning. Religion in all its forms tends to have a dual character.

Let me illustrate that by reference to a television program from the time when talk shows and panels were new inventions. In 1959, Americans were just learning the "Protestant, Catholic, and Jew" scheme and were treating each other with caution. Still, this was the Eisenhower era, when there was a widely noted revival of religious interest in the culture. These were tense times in the Cold War, and Americans were trying to determine what was distinctive about "their side." Religion, they largely agreed, was a major part of it. Just five years before, Congress had inserted the words "under God" in the Pledge of Allegiance. The legislature did this because on paper, both the Soviet Union and the United States, chief antagonists in the Cold War, professed to be republics, to love democracy, and to guarantee freedoms. But the Soviet government would not want to be "under God."

So religion was in the air, but it was on the airwaves only in very protected forms. Chief among these was the Sunday morning panel operated by the large faith families. They avoided delicate subjects.

Along came David Susskind with a program called *Open End*. One Sunday, this host summoned six of us young commentators on religion—Protestant, Catholic, Jew, atheist—to converse and argue indefinitely into the night (the end of the show was indeed "open").

We were invited to discuss "religion in America." That Sunday, as we boarded planes for New York and the studio, we read in the *New York Times* that these six people would be discussing "fear and prejudice in America." When the show started, someone—I believe it was William F. Buckley Jr.—asked, "Why the switch? What happened to *religion* in the title?" Susskind, blushing, answered, roughly as I recall it now, "Because if we use the word *religion*, half the potential audience would think it will be too boring and the other half will think it's too dangerous."

Today, religion gets treated more frequently and with more depth than it was forty years and more ago. But something of that concern—too boring or too dangerous—remains. And even to think about it can cause school leadership to hesitate. Given the hurdles before us, there are temptations to give up on all efforts. Giving up, however, brings with it some liabilities about which Americans may profitably converse.

Religion's Place in the Public Schools

The proper study of religion in public elementary schools contributes to the common good. This is true for several reasons.

First, studying religion helps achieve the goal of public schooling: students will learn a more accurate picture of the world around them. In a culture that is anything but secular, religion belongs in the curriculum. With religious knowledge in hand, students will be able to account for a wider and deeper range of human motivation and action.

This is true in many different ways. Religion inspired most of the great art centuries ago and even now it informs much artistic expression. The stories, myths, symbols, and poetry of religion and its scriptures can enhance imaginations. From studying religion children may learn wonder and therefore to approach nature, neighbor, and self with more depth and appreciation than they could without it. Students can begin, on children's levels, to formulate more reasons why people act morally, why some respond to a call to "do justice, love mercy, and walk humbly." A picture of the moral dimensions of life painted without religion is incomplete. With religion as a part of public education, children may learn of some dangers to avoid, and they can gain perspective on the faiths or nonfaiths they and their neighbors practice.

Urging the proper study of religion in public schools also means including the study of sacred texts, not as propaganda but as literature. Those equipped with the knowledge of the Hebrew scriptures and the New Testament will understand significantly more literary allusions in European and North American (including African American) literature than otherwise. They can better understand the rituals of various communities, especially as these are often portrayed on television during the republic's times of trials and triumphs. Children can learn how and why faith communities share narratives that inspire civil action and voluntary associations. As they study religion, students will read stories of intrinsic value and acquire more resources that explicate the human condition.

Making religion a part of public education can also make students aware of the sometimes negative aspects of religious faith. Without biasing children against religion, teachers and texts can help explain the mixed consequences of religious faith. Stories of Heaven's Gate, Jonestown, or Waco may be too graphic for younger students, but often these children will see such groups portrayed on television and are bereft of interpretive tools. Children can pick up some of these critical tools without coaching or coaxing from teachers. On their own, they may have begun to assemble their own do-it-yourself kits for spiritual detective work. With an understanding of the religious undergirdings of moral claims and impulses, students might begin to line up more intelligently on public policy issues like foreign aid, development, or military intervention. In short, religion is too important an aspect of human existence, and especially the American circumstance, to be left out of public education.

The High Costs of Giving Up

Suppose that you are an advocate for teaching "about" religion in public schools. Someone asks you what would be missing if the schools did *not* do such teaching. She follows up by asking what positive things students would learn that would prepare them for life. What would you say? I would respond, "screen out such religious teaching and learning if you wish, but think of the educational costs."

Won't children benefit from more honest accountings of the American and other stories—stories that are biased in the cases when something as important as religion gets slighted, obscured, or even deliberately excluded? The proper formula is something like this: where religion is relevant to a story or theme, it should be brought into the open and receive fair treatment. In most cases, to avoid controversy, schools have too often avoided religion entirely, thereby distorting certain themes and miseducating children.

If there is to be no separate discipline or hour or strategy that addresses religion, religion belongs in the schools on the principle of "natural inclusion." The principle of natural inclusion is dead-set against "unnatural exclusion." When textbooks, curriculum planners, and teachers ignore events, personalities, and arguments that are incompletely explained with reference to religion, this runs counter to the goals of public education. Speak about faith and spirituality where the topic naturally fits—which is not everywhere but still plenty of places.

One example is the civil rights movement in twentieth-century America. Often writers treat it as a political force based on secular ideals. But while there certainly were secular-minded leaders and no shortages of pragmatic politicking, many of the movement's leadership and workers were explicitly inspired by religion. It was not an accident that a key group's name was the Southern *Christian* Leadership Conference and that many of the movement's leaders were called "Reverend"—King, Abernathy, Young, Walker, Shuttlesworth, Bevel, Jackson, and others, twenty-deep. These civil rights leaders appealed to the quasi-religious aspects of the Declaration of Independence and the U.S. Constitution, but they drew equally on a reservoir of religious faith that most Americans professed to follow. They chided and rallied citizens by citing the Hebrew scriptures, the New Testament teachings of Jesus and Paul, and more contemporary religious leaders from Howard Thurman to Gandhi. To deal with the civil rights movement while excluding religion deprives students of the full substance and context of the story.

We can think of many other liabilities to excluding religion from education. Will children be adequately prepared to find their places in a global culture, where different religious outlooks color everything from economic transactions to motivations for war? Will children understand what motivates most charitable giving and activity in American society? If they do not understand this, will they be less motivated themselves to aid charities or do volunteer work?

Even more questions follow, all of them important. Will children be able to make sense of the literature, art, and music of the past, all of which prominently feature religion? In the contemporary world, will they fully understand current devotion to broadly defined religious themes in movies and other public expressions? Will children be able to ground themselves in debates about morality, virtues, life philosophies?

Will children fully grasp the depths and heights of the human story, so that they can interpret these and then assist others in searching for meaning or becoming liberated? Will they be haunted by or inspired by signals from others very different from themselves? Will they be at home with politics in a time when campaigners and legislators have become more explicit about their own religious motivations or more up-front in dealing with religiously motivated constituencies? Will they really have a basic and complete understanding of their own local communities, particularly as ever more religious groups grow articulate?

These questions are only a beginning. In mixed company, more and more examples will be brought forward. If participants choose to follow the ground rules of argument, picture conflict and an early breakup of the circle. If they follow the rules of conversation, in which questions, not answers, dominate, expect curiosity, hilarity, creativity, and insight to emerge—often among citizens who least expect that they have something to offer.

6

The Religious Schooling Response

We picture all thoughtful citizens engaged with the subject of public education. Some mistrust education by others so much that they home-school; some teach their children at home because they are natural teachers and believe that they can offer something special to their children. Yet all will still look out the window and over the wall to see what is happening in public education. Affirm it or despise it, they must care.

With what is called private and especially parochial education, we come to a special case. Public school advocates sometimes dismiss parochial education out of hand because it *is* parochial. (*Parochial* refers to education related to religion and religious institutions.) They wonder whether education informed by religious faith can be "open" and healthy. Others will be indifferent to parochial education: what other people do is their business, and if some want to pass up public schools and pay for alternatives, that is their business. Still others mildly applaud, having heard that inner-city parochial education is more effective than most public education in particular places. That there is a religious impulse behind the education matters little; what counts is the product, and parochial students have often proved themselves to be superior products.

A harder case to make is the parallel notion that in a republic, parochial education *is* public, a concern of the public. In other words, private educational institutions bear on the public order. Although in this book we pay the most attention to public education at the primary, secondary, and university levels, we also want to make the case that public-minded people should care about what happens in nonpublic schools.

Caring About What Happens in Nonpublic Schools

Contemporary cultural conflicts have nineteenth-century antecedents, many more violent than any we know today. In the middle of the nineteenth century, as Catholic immigration increased, Protestant anti-Catholicism grew militant. Unthinking (or maybe cunning) Protestant leaders in the common school movement used only the King James Version of the Bible—not the Catholics' choice—so Catholics established parochial schools, in part to keep their distance. From the middle of the nineteenth century on, many hundreds of thousands of children were drawn into parochial schools and away from tax-supported, locally authorized education. It was there, in local common schools, where the larger community's values and meanings were passed along to new generations.

Catholics were not alone in going on their own. Some Lutherans and other well-defined religious groups, especially those who wanted to preserve languages they brought from Europe, started parochial schools as well. They wanted to use languages as guardians of ethnic cohesiveness and as aids in perpetuating distinctive cultures and religious orthodoxies. They did not want to share religious meanings with the common schools, especially since they discerned that these common schools thrived on religious philosophies alien to the newcomers.

The parochial school people knew that they were "other" to the public schools, so they responded in kind. So did some Seventh-day Adventists, Quakers, Amish, and others. All prefigured those who in recent years set up evangelical schools as alternatives to public schools, which are too inattentive to their own rights and traditions. Their withdrawal, then as now, did not mean that they were disloyal or unpatriotic. They liked being in America, and by and large they celebrated American achievements and wholeheartedly participated in America's struggles. But they had their own interpretations of what was going on.

These nineteenth-century inventions show that the entire public has not always equally accepted the public schools. Meanwhile, modern-day criticisms of the "myth of the common school" have demonstrated that all kinds of religious messages are telegraphed and transported in the public sphere by people who may not have recognized the particular nature of those sentiments.

Today, most parochial education is under one of two auspices. The larger context, Catholic education, faces problems and is experiencing some decline. The other, evangelical education, has rapidly and steadily grown in the past three decades. (Of course, Lutherans, Episcopalians, Friends, and Adventists also operate parochial schools, but their public dimensions resemble those of the two larger groups.) Whoever thinks the American future will be decided without reference to the Catholic and evangelical quarters of the population will probably care little about their forms of education. But those who recognize the potency of Catholicism and evangelicalism in public life have good reason to read further.

The Public Dimensions of Private Schooling

Nowadays, voucher plans focus the debate over public and private schooling, causing controversy and quickening public concern. Whatever else they do, vouchers provide tax relief for parents who choose private or parochial schools. Whether or not the public ultimately decides in favor of vouchers, it is still appropriate to ask just what is public about private education. It will be most profitable to restrict the discussion to private schools run by religious groups, since this is where and when issues of religion arise. And presumably, if the case for vouchers is credible for parochial schooling, secular private schools will easily be included in voucher plans.

Religiously related schools have long faced opposition on at least two fronts. From one side, secular-minded citizens have taken offense at the very existence of religious schools and all that they do and represent. The public school, they argue, is the common school, designed to integrate various immigrant children into American culture. Every institution independent of such schools threatens to divide citizens and fails to prepare children adequately for full and enthusiastic citizenship in the republic.

From the other side, advocates of a generalized civic faith, civil religion, or public religion find parochial schools too sectarian and too self-enclosed to serve societal purposes. In the days before the Second Vatican Council (1962–1965), when anti-Catholicism was the stock-in-trade of many mainline and liberal Protestants, Catholic schools were virulently attacked. Such assaults became rare after the council, when both Catholic schools and perceptions of them changed. But in the 1950s, some people made a profession of attacking Catholic schools not for being religious but for being religious in the wrong way. One figure in particular, Paul Blanshard, regularly issued book-length attacks on Catholicism and its perceived threat to religious freedom. Faithful Catholics, in his eyes, were menaces to liberty, and parochial schools were the dangerous training grounds for these subversives.[1]

Forty years later, Catholic and other church-related schools increasingly escaped criticism from secularists, church-state sentries, and other religious believers. So long as their leaders did not press too hard for tax-exemption plans or relief programs, they were no longer a target. Instead, the evangelical and fundamentalist schools now awakened suspicion and hostility. Their teachers and parents, according to critics, professed worldviews that were uncongenial to the rest of America. Parents in the South, resisting school desegregation, invented some of these evangelical academies, making them obvious targets for individuals who wanted to attack religious conservatives.

Criticism of Parochial Education: A Case Study

Now and then, critics will combine the two motives and issue a general polemic. Legal scholar James G. Dwyer has penned one such work, *Religious Schools v. Children's Rights*, in which he offers a sustained attack on parochial education that brings together many of the piecemeal criticisms of such schools and thus it is worthy of attention.[2]

From the beginning, Dwyer views parochial education as an entity that tramples the rights of children. These schools indoctrinate the young and promulgate views that are incongruent with and subversive of the larger public good.

In pursuing his case, Dwyer draws on material from two main sources. The first source, a study of girls and women, stressed their need to recover from parochial education in order to gain self-esteem and gender equity. How could Dwyer know that parochial schools had inflicted such damage? He described testimony from adults who had had bad experiences in Catholic childhood.

Dwyer's other source is a series of books on "testimonies" from former fundamentalists, which detail matters such as the self-enclosed character of the religious schools they attended and the moral intensity that leads them to be hostile to much of American public life. The author had no difficulty finding many teachings and practices that most citizens consider suspicious or repulsive.

Dwyer does not do any comparing, leaving aside the parochial schools in other religious traditions and the more ecumenically open Catholic schools that are increasingly common. He makes no reference to the thousands upon thousands of contented

"survivors" of Catholic parochial education. He includes no bib-
liography of testimonies of individuals explaining how Catholic
education had made them better American citizens and had
sparked their commitment to volunteer service. Dwyer offers no
original research on evangelical schools or what went on inside
them, simply trusting other scholars and putting their conclusions
to his own purposes. Dwyer has a point to make, a theme to carry,
and a thesis to enforce, and he pushes all other questions out of
the way.

Dwyer remains concerned chiefly with children's educational
rights, including their right to escape what he sees as a too-sheltered
environment. His critics, in turn, can note that he cedes all rights
to the government, as the controlling authority of the schools. State
officials, and no others, must determine what is best for a child.
They set all the terms of the educational environment with an eye
toward producing students who fit into the larger culture. Dwyer's
pages reveal no sense that some people better serve society by questioning its assumptions rather than falling into line.

We write this as people who personally may not find congenial
many features of parochial education, and it is a fair target for certain criticisms. But the issue here is whether it is appropriate to con-
demn, a priori, schools whose philosophy and ethos differ from some
presumed societal consensus about public education.

Dwyer's indictment of parochial education appears in the subheadings throughout his book, and they pretty well summarize the
historic arguments against Catholic education before Catholicism
became more mainstream. These subheadings also reproduce the
contemporary civil libertarian critique of the more separatist evangelical academies. We cite these section titles in order to prompt
further inquiry, for conversation around a civic table. What is the
case Dwyer makes against parochial schools? Here we reproduce the
topical skeleton from his first chapter, "Catholic and Fundamentalist Schooling Today":[3]

Certainly, these can be features of any school system. But it is not easy to picture non-Catholic inner-city parents of Catholic school–attending children describing the parochial schools their children attend in this way. They know that their children will obtain a superior education in a healthy environment and that their children are unlikely to feel pressure to convert to Catholicism. As for the graduates, each child altered by the parochial school experience can become an agent of the civic good.

Dwyer naturally criticizes the courts, who have often favored the rights of parents over those of children. How can this situation be reversed? Dwyer suggests new legislation, which he quite rightly and realistically foresees as generating "fierce resistance." Dwyer argues that he does not completely oppose voucher systems, but alternative schools simply must be transformed until "children in religious schools enjoy the same legal protections that children in public schools enjoy, and enjoy equal educational opportunity." He urges citizens to work for change in this direction, until "the legal foundation on which the institution of religious schooling in its present form now rests will begin to crumble."[4]

We may have overdone criticizing Dwyer and underplayed some subtleties in his argument in the interest of presenting a clearly defined position against which other theorists can react. What writers from Blanshard to Dwyer have successfully done is this: they have forced advocates of private and parochial schools to make the case for their public functions. This does not mean that such schools exist *only* for such uses, but it does mean that when challenged, alternative schools must examine how they perform on this front.

Religious Schools as Public Schools

Leaving aside evangelical academies, where there is more diversity, we turn now to ask whether or not Catholic schools *are* public schools. In the face of generalizations like those of Dwyer, it is an important question to pose. From the Catholic side, support for religious schools will depend a bit on one's conception of their purposes. From the public side, perceptions of the role of religious schools will change in light of their function.

Perhaps the issue is better defined by asking the opposite question: In what way are parochial schools *not* public? The answer involves ownership. Parochial schools lie outside the structures of taxation and government. Also, religious schools are not public in that children in the sponsoring denomination usually have the inside track on enrollment and tuition breaks. Only in these two respects is most parochial education, by definition, not public.

Do special issues arise because there is public use without public ownership? Naturally. Catholic educators set most of the policies, just as various public entities do for public schools. And of course, the whole issue of funding occurs at the point where public meets private. Most private schools are financially pinched at a time when costs—for laboratories, texts, teacher salaries—are all on the rise, often beyond the ordinary means of sponsoring churches and other religious organizations.

Having said that, the question arises, why care about the way we conceive of schools, in this case religious schools, and their relationship to the public order? The answer here is because conceptions matter. Basic values about education and society are at issue, and they will do much to shape the future. Also, citizens must come to perceive their society and its institutions accurately. Thus if the Nation of Islam teaches black separatism in its schools, the state has no business intervening unless it detects public violence behind that philosophy. Citizens can find independent ways to criticize and oppose views with which they disagree, but they cannot call on the state to suppress them.

Great changes have made Catholic parochial schools look more public. Before the Second Vatican Council inspired so many changes, there was still a reality called the "Catholic ghetto." Most Catholics then tended to live in worlds designed to be organic, integral, figuratively walled in and separated from the larger public. The Catholic ghettos, generally defensive toward the culture's influence, are now gone. Children, parents, and teachers in Catholic schools are now very much a part of American culture. Non-Catholic attitudes have undergone a corresponding transformation.

Catholic theologies of education and of the relationship between church and society have changed drastically, so Catholic schools have come to be dedicated to positive support of many values in the larger society. Where once parochial schools were seen to be proselytizing agencies, now they respect others' outlooks. This attitude includes friendliness toward African American Baptist, Pentecostal, and Methodist communities in the neighborhoods Catholic schools serve.

In such areas, and even in affluent suburbs, Catholic schools are no longer alien but are a substantial part of mainstream culture. Yet they can also offer alternative educational models and worldviews. This is a social good for all except those who find the model of public education near perfect.

To pursue this further, we have to ask, what makes a school public? We can cite several elements. There must be an openness, a positive view of sources beyond the school's context. All private education may be infused with a particular theology and ethos, but it cannot be *only* that if it is to be public. In each parochial situation that would be public, there must be some consideration of sources beyond the believing community. For example, a conservative Christian school would consciously show interest in alternative philosophies. If parochial schools close themselves off from any such influences, they still would have the right to exist, but they would be sectarian, cloistered, nonpublic.

While some American religious communities hold negative views of public order and human learning, most theological traditions seek positive engagement. They put energies into the community. They want to produce the best possible citizens, not just for life with fellow-believers in the sanctuary but also in the marketplace and the public forum. This means that parochial school graduates somehow relate to worldviews beyond their own, thought-systems that are in play in the public arena. Parochial school graduates then exist on their own terms but also as citizens in a plural American context.

There is no single Catholic, Episcopal, Lutheran, or evangelical philosophy of education that animates all the schools in a system. Denominations contain considerable internal differences. Yet overall, these schools all offer interpretations of how God works in a mixed and pluralist society. They seek to discern how to work cooperatively with voters and leaders who may have different worldviews.

Private schools often have constituencies that are *more*, not less, diverse than the public schools. The tax-supported institutions usually reflect the social class and the relative racial or ethnic homo-geneity of each neighborhood. Private schools, by contrast, often draw on far-flung constituencies. They often feel called, for religious reasons, to attract students from various ethnic groups, and they often succeed in diversifying their student bodies far more than public schools do.

For this reason, such schools can be laboratories for developing citizenship, one sensitive to many worldviews and not channeled through public authorities. At their best, these schools help prepare children for participation in a diverse, vibrant culture. At the same time, they also train students for life in subcommunities that make their own positive contributions to the common good.

If anything, Catholic schools of old and evangelical schools today could most accurately be criticized for being overly patriotic, overly eager to prove their Americanness to all who look in on them. John Tracy Ellis in *American Catholicism* compared the old-style Catholic patriot to certain guards in the prerevolutionary court: "Half suspect—they bow too low."[5] At their best, however, they teach students to be critically loyal and loyally critical in the society and nation around them.

We have here underplayed prophetic roles that belong in public religion, but they are there, as they have been since the time of Jeremiah. Parochial education at its best can, in effect, say to staff and students, celebrate and participate in the public order as we might, there comes a time when we must say no to this or that public policy. Faith communities, at least in intention, put boundaries around politics and its kin. Politics, a crucial human construct, can serve creative and necessary purposes, but politically active citizens are often tempted toward self-aggrandizement, chauvinism, and a nationalist spirit that drowns out internal criticism. In modest ways, parochial education can help apply the brakes to such negative temptations, helping citizens understand their vocations in a wider context.

The Private Nature of Home Schooling

In most discussions of religion and education, the subject of home schooling will draw more attention than it has here. It is difficult to comment on home schooling from the perspective of the public order because motivations differ so drastically. As noted, sometimes parents home-school because they are educators who want to put their pedagogical skills to work in service of their own children. Others may have a particular philosophical outlook—pacifist, ecological, communitarian, religious—that does not match public education's general intention. Home schooling allows parents to create and control the educational environment and course content to support their goals.

Home schooling can also be seen as the penultimate form of rejecting the present public order (*no* education would be the ultimate form). Such rejection can be born of mistrusting the consequences of interacting with differently minded others. It can be a means of disdaining an education system perceived as eroding proper values, morals, virtues, character, and faith. Sometimes home schooling can represent a rejection of both public and private education because by removing the child from the home, both systems conspire to erode group boundaries in the service of educating for citizenship. When the home boundaries are impenetrable, when the neighbors are kept at a safe distance, when the antennae for societal signals collapse, describing any positive dimension to the relationship between home schooling and the public becomes impossible.

Parents who educate their children at home may argue that they are producing superior citizens for the kingdom of heaven or that they are generating critics of the present public order. What will always be lacking in such private schooling is direct, person-to-person interaction with individuals with other worldviews, whether students, teachers, parents, or other constituencies.

Certainly, some home schooling may be designed with the specific intention of producing better American citizens. Critics may say this sounds oxymoronic, but thousands of parents make the case that it is indeed possible to do so. Though statistically rather small, this growing sector represents a negation of the wider society's terms, and its products will tend to become and remain defensive in a culture that might welcome their witness and example if they moved in it freely. Yet by the very fact of its existence, this private-looking home-schooling movement carries messages to those who care about public education and public religion alike.

7

Church-Related Higher Education
and the Common Good

In this chapter, we turn to private colleges and universities, especially if they are labeled "church-related" or if they consciously seek to treat religion in the public sphere.

So specialized, so settled into grooves are we—and I *do* include myself—that sometimes its is hard to entertain new ways of thinking about certain subjects. But as I've urged throughout this book, issues of religion and republic demand a seamless, integrated, multilevel view of education. This holds true now that we have private institutions of higher education in our sights. Although this subject may at first glance seem quite specialized, I hope you will give me a chance to make my case once again.

The word *private* can be taken to mean "keep out!" or "hands off!" or "none of your business" or "trespassers will be prosecuted." And on the surface, such lines are in place. The free exercise clause of the First Amendment secures the right for citizens to determine their own religious preferences. So, one might ask, who besides Latter-day Saints should care about what Mormons do at their Brigham Young University? Who besides evangelicals should care what happens at Wheaton College? Should anyone but Catholics pay attention to what goes on at Catholic University of America?

These questions can be answered in several ways, but which is the right one? No one at all should care? The very few should be interested? The tens of millions of citizens who are heavily invested in private higher education? The many millions who are involved with religion? Or everybody? Here is the case for *everybody*.

The Case for Common Involvement for the Common Good

To be sure, private colleges and universities—those academies not directly under governmental control or directly dependent on tax funds—do represent a relatively small and dwindling percentage of higher education investments, expenditures, enrollments, and energies. They are small in number, relatively speaking: amass the millions of dollars in all of higher education, and these vital church-related colleges would represent a tiny portion of the whole enterprise. Yet included in this sector are many of America's most prestigious and influential institutions of higher education: the Ivy League schools and the Stanfords and Chicagos across the land. These are the schools that have so much to do with shaping American science, policy, and imagination. And this sector also includes fundamentalist and Pentecostal Bible colleges, which train the elite of both powerful, conservative religious organizations and assertive political movements that have a bearing on public life. How all of these institutions relate to public life and religion matter greatly for the present and future of our culture.

At the undergraduate level, private-sector schools prepare an inordinately high percentage of the nation's eventual graduate students, guiding them as they go about choosing which professions to enter. What attitudes will these graduates have with respect to basic issues of life? How will they contribute as citizens to civil life in this republic? What will they think and do with respect to the market economy? To the voluntary sector? To humanitarian needs? It concerns all of us how other citizens, who may not share all our values, answer such questions.

One might reasonably ask, what difference does it make to the sponsors of private schools if citizens at large take an interest in their endeavors? In such halls and laboratories, citizens train for jobs and secure tools that enable them to make a living. In these settings, citizens prepare for professions where they can engage in informed activity that purports to serve human good—and be paid for it. Students at private institutions are more likely than their public university counterparts to do some of their undergraduate learning in other nations or to be involved in service projects around the world. This means that they are already ambassadors, transmitting knowledge to and about other places. Given all that, the questions concerning sponsors and their stewardship are important.

In such schools, students can refine their callings, their vocations, in the light of special resources made available or distinctive attitudes cultivated in the classroom, in the library, and in interaction with others. There, though not only in this kind of school, they confront the great humanistic achievements of the past and the troubling issues of the present. They probe the meanings of citizenship and the transactions of market and republic. Students pursue or are encouraged to pursue philosophies of life appropriate for individuals and the larger society. They engage in research that can enhance individual and communal life in a wide variety of ways. Such observations as these barely scratch the surface, suggesting how urgent it is to ponder issues not only of higher education in general but also of the realm of private and church-related institutions in particular.

Still not convinced? Consider an analogy or two. I may not be a stockholder in a private company that manufactures arms and explosives, yet I will care about what issues from that company. I may not invest in a profit-driven medical center, but it concerns me whether or not it follows proper guidelines on human experimentation and is otherwise ethically accountable. Ideas have consequences, consequences that kill or heal people. Because explosive ideas arise in collegiate settings, all of us should care about the people and institutions that generate them and about the graduates who carry these ideas forth into the republic we all inhabit.

None of this means that we citizens are called on to be amateur accrediting agencies, sleuths, snoops, or spies. Higher academia is a technical minefield through which to walk, representing a set of specialties that people with other specialties are often not in a position to appraise. But this should not prevent us from taking an overall interest in the mission and intention of higher education on all fronts. What these institutions do ultimately affects us all.

So we forthrightly take up questions dealing especially with those colleges and universities that somehow have links with institutional religion. No matter what your location in the republic or your view of religion in public life, we bid all of you to initiate conversations on this subject.

Connections Between Religion and Higher Education

Throughout this chapter, we will use the expression "church-related" to refer to all institutions of higher education with religious ties, including colleges and universities with Jewish, Buddhist, Muslim, or other denominational connections. The overwhelming majority of these institutions are Christian, of course, and so the word *church* serves as a convenient shorthand. In this private sector, hundreds of institutions can be identified as "church-related" in some way.

These schools incorporate a wide variety of church relations. Father Richard McCormick once addressed a question to Catholic hospitals: "If you were to be indicted for being Catholic, would there be enough evidence to convict you?" This question, slightly adapted, serves as a good way to evaluate the strength of ties between religious groups and church-related colleges. If accused of having a particular religious connection, would there be enough evidence to convict them?

The answer, of course, depends on the school examined, as well as on who is answering the question. At some institutions, the religious tie is apparent and strong, and a church-inspired impulse is part of the school's mission. At other places, the old religious ties, once vivid, are now mere vestiges, all but buried like fossils in earlier strata of experience. In such cases, the religious connections may not be vital to the school's current mission. But whether still intimate or almost forgotten, these connections between private institutions and religion help determine a whole set of philosophical questions that concern us all.

Most of you who take up this topic will find that there is a need, first of all, to differentiate between kinds of colleges in this sector. Picturing all schools in this zone as identical only causes confusion, for there are some very real differences among them. But if we view them all from the angle of their actual and potential contributions to the public religion scene, they would appear on a spectrum between these two poles.

At one end of the spectrum, a certain set of church-related schools has it almost too easy in trying to keep religion central—thanks to their ownership, their governing boards, their constituencies, their hiring policies, and the students they attract. Attend a determinedly evangelical school where leaders fear the school might slip down the slippery slope of secularization, as so many Catholic and mainstream Protestant schools already have, and you will find that the school's concentration is directed inward. Faculty and students sign statements of faith that are so restrictive that they keep others at a safe distance. No one is permitted to teach at some such schools unless they affirm the inerrancy and infallibility of the Bible, including what it has to say about science and nature. Evangelical scholars who have spread their wings some and found biblical reasons to back up a bit from the notion of biblical inerrancy know that they stand no chance of getting tenure if they do not subscribe to the college's statement of faith. But signing on leads them to second-class status in the company of most biblical scholars, who have a predilection for literary and historical approaches to sacred texts.

Evangelicals can run into the same trouble at ultraconservative schools when it comes to the teaching of evolution. If presented at all, in these settings it often must be accompanied by the teaching of "scientific creationism," which seeks to square literal biblical accounts of creation with scientific theory and observation. Disagreeing with evolution tends to rule such a creationist school out of serious contention in scientific circles. In these church-related settings, individuals in other disciplines may feel betrayed, stigmatized, and unfairly discredited. Books published by their science and religion departments may express a sense of alienation from and hostility toward other worldviews, greatly reducing the size of the public such writings will reach.

With the wagons circled against the hostility of such colleagues, it is tempting for these evangelicals to develop a negative, even paranoid view of the larger world. And it is easy for academics "out there" to dismiss conservative church-related schools as mere thought-control centers. When evangelical schools erect such barriers and define such boundaries, they rule out many individuals who share most features of their faith and theology.

Professors in other colleges sometimes joke about the evasions that occur when the walls are built too high. We have heard of a literature teacher at Evangelical U., where all tenure-track faculty must sign a statement of faith that begins something like this: "Evangelical U. believes in the inerrancy of the Bible, in all matters of nature, science, and history." The literature professor has signed the statement. A skeptical friend asks, "How could you sign? You have a high view of biblical authority, but you don't agree with the scholastic propositions that stand behind that affirmation.

Where's your integrity?" The answer: "No problem. I did sign it. Because *I believe that* Evangelical U. believes all that." The punch line evokes a smile, but not on the faces of scientific establishments, evangelicals with more open views, or enforcers of the codes.

The point about church-related schools at this end of the spectrum is that they have little problem with their own *religion* but a great number of problems with the *public*.

At the other end of the spectrum are church-related schools that have drifted so far from their religious roots that those ties have been all but severed. These schools also present problems, albeit of a different sort, for engagement with public religion. Let us take several examples.

One such school, widely lauded as "excellent," may have won its way into acceptance by the public and the academic community as well. It may be a Catholic school, one whose leadership and much of its constituency is at home with Catholic teaching. It keeps its guard up and demonstrates caution only by avoiding overt campus endorsements of birth control or by muting any rejection of full-blown views of papal infallibility. In the working out of academic affairs, this school's leaders may have left their Catholic distinctives so far behind that the Catholic, Christian, and religious dimensions of learning become more problematic in many disciplines than gaining public acceptance ever could be.

At a conference on academic freedom and the religious college in 1998, this wide spectrum was visible. The event's sponsors, the American Association of University Professors (AAUP), invited a wide range of college representatives. One set—evangelical and conservative Lutheran and Reformed Protestants—told stories of heresy accusations at their institutions. In some cases, professors were denied tenure in disputes over doctrinal matters. The schools were tied up with tensions over proper theological interpretations and risked losing their accreditation, all because many colleagues found their religious definitions too precise and their enforcement too rigorous. Of course, to most people at the conference and to the AAUP, all these issues and incidents represented problems of academic freedom and integrity. Such church-related schools risked being perceived as marginal, self-enclosed, merely private and confessional.

In the same room, representatives of many mainstream Protestant, Lutheran, and Catholic schools could not recall any similar instances. They could not remember any heresy trials or even intimations that there should be some. These people and their schools were completely at home in the world of academic accreditation, accepted by their secular peers. Of course, in the minds of the conservatives, this raised the question as to whether the religious vision might have perished in the interest of satisfying the demands of the wider culture. Should there be no tension at all, they may have asked their peers, between culture and church, between Athens and Jerusalem?

In our volatile culture, matters are never so simple as this polarity suggests. At the conference, both sides were shocked to hear of a particular challenge to intellectual freedom in a liberal Protestant academic context. A chaplain at a university connected with United Methodism had conducted a blessing or marriage ceremony for a gay couple. Many in the church body protested this as a violation of the denomination's official position and demanded that the chaplain be punished as if he were a minister in a congregation. Evidently, loose and fading church ties on campus can still have consequences, but only if acts are vividly "scandalous," too obviously out of step with constituent interests.

Another situation, in American Catholicism, illustrates the complexity of reality between the two poles. The Vatican has issued *Ex corde ecclesia*, a decree that puts Catholic schools under some greater measure of church control. If American Catholic bishops strictly interpret this decree, say its critics, true academic freedom at Catholic universities would come to an end. At a future AAUP conference on the subject, Catholic institutions would not be in the "home free" category. The issue may be resolved, but there are signs of persistent tension.

These examples of warring orthodoxies and disputed conformities further reveal the dimensions to which church-related institutions of higher education deal with issues that have public consequences. Although they do not constitute a large proportion of higher education as a whole, schools in this sector will continue to influence the shape of life in the republic. And the place of church-related colleges is not a settled issue.

Key Issues and Contemporary Challenges

To hear from people "in the trenches," we invited a circle of academics responsible for church-related schools to gather around a huge table and converse. These leaders from religion-related academies included faculty and administrators, theologians and cultural commentators, educational theorists and public policy experts. We played the role of amateur ethnographers and took notes on what they reported. Several common themes and challenges emerged, and their subjects can become yours as you create your own tables around which to carry on conversation.

As with most institutions these days, church-related colleges are urgently grappling with the question of *identity*. Most of these schools "look like America," in all its pluralist glory. These institutions appear from some angles to be almost entirely adapted to the norms of secular colleges. Policies, accreditation, faculty hiring, classroom methods, and the mix of students are so similar to those at schools without religious ties that in some cases the stipulation that the college president must be Lutheran or Presbyterian is all that distinguishes them anymore.

Questions come. Should these schools not try to regain at least some distance from the larger culture, at least some differences from other kinds of schools? Should they not attempt to demonstrate some measure of alienation from the wider culture and its purely secular schools? Should this goal not be part of a church-related institution's renewed sense of mission and identity?

This question of identity remains difficult to address because people outside the orbit of church-related higher education are also asking the same question. Many members of the public have little understanding of this combination between religion and private colleges, further complicating the way they expect this question to be resolved. A church-inspired college, however thin the connection between church and college has become, is at least chartered to explore and teach what religion is, what goes into it, and how it functions. But will the public recognize this? Will the students and alumni of such schools be aware of their particular intentions and articulate this?

A related question concerns the bifocal and bilingual nature of church-related institutions of higher education. "What has Athens to do with Jerusalem?" asked a pious church father, wondering what the worlds of knowledge and faith really have to do with each other. The leaders and supporters in church-related colleges ask and answer this age-old question in new forms. There should always be some uneasiness with respect to the relation between learning and faith, many will argue, for Athens and Jerusalem operate with different intents and measures.

Identity questions play out further in the reciprocal relationships between campus administrators and sponsoring religious groups. One college chaplain reported that at her school, daily life reveals hardly any awareness of churchly ties or origins. Most students remain almost totally ignorant of the inherited connections and possible implications. Colleges with religious connections may tend to exemplify the same kind of relativism that characterizes comparable public colleges: all worldviews are equal. Yet, this same chaplain reports, there *is* in fact a quickening of spiritual searches on this kind of campus, one that mirrors that in the general culture. Some of that searching is encouraged by religious studies faculty on the academic side and by the presence of a chapel, chaplain, and spirituality forums on the other.

Another chaplain observed that today there are especially intense and refined *studies* of religion. Although interest in religious practices had long been dissipating, courses that proposed to study religion are quite popular, evoking widespread student interest. Do such studies take on any special character because they take place in a private, religiously inspired school? Or would students down the block at the state university reveal similar interests and curiosities?

The subject of religion and education soon intersects with the cultural trend concerning "spirituality," and this zone is no exception. In one of our conversations, a leader at a college founded in the last half century on aggressively secular grounds noted that some vestigial sense of religious responsibility led to the provision of a chapel and a chaplaincy. After tragedies occurred—a student's death, a natural disaster, a military conflict like the Gulf War, the destruction of the space shuttle *Challenger*, the murder of a gay student—chapels at this and similar "secular" institutions were crowded. Students who have not known to practice, or *how* to practice, a faith now seek at least the space in which spiritual searches take place.

This college leader contrasted this wan and occasional aspect of campus expression with experiences at church-related institutions. There, especially at one Jesuit-sponsored school, a passion for social justice was consistent, concentrated, encouraged, and related explicitly to the school's religious mission. But Catholic advocates in the heterogeneous student body showed respect for and appealed to students who might pursue justice on other grounds. It is easier to mobilize students around visions of justice, this chaplain argued, where some specific language of faith had been developed and remained current.

One leader of a religiously connected college noted that today's students find terms like *spirituality* congenial but reject any sense of denominational commitment. With the encouragement of that school's leadership, we heard, some of the familiar forms of communal energy now get transferred into highly motivated commitments to voluntary associations. Through these groups, students and the schools themselves have their most immediate impact on surrounding publics, and schools expect that their graduates will continue this emphasis after they leave.

Meanwhile, the most visible and vital groups on college campuses tend to be the more conservative evangelical groups like the Inter-Varsity Christian Fellowship, Campus Crusade for Christ, and Fellowship of Christian Athletes. Catholic and mainstream Protestant groups, whose theologies are often closer to that of a school's founding denomination, fade into the background in many places. That trend demands and deserves discussion.

Some readers may think that scholars at church-related schools may have "settled" for such places while preferring positions at unattached secular institutions. Yet many do choose church-related higher education over other alternatives, whether or not they share all aspects of an institution's vision and mission. One conversation partner indicated that he taught in such a context precisely because he remained committed to a variety of publics, and he could nurture them at such a place. But this can be effective and rewarding only if colleges are perceived to be excellent places of learning.

Another conversation partner, from what he called an "open-minded" evangelical school, spoke of the fate of liberal arts at church-related schools. His school prizes humanities, social sciences, and service vocations, and the institution's leaders take pains to ensure that it stays within its tradition and its strengths. At the same time, the school is making efforts to broaden its scope, ecumenically speaking. It welcomes an ever more diverse student body that is attracted and committed to a generally evangelical vision.

Perhaps in reaction to suggestions that such a school cannot be academically first-rate or perhaps nudged by its own faculty to recognize that evangelicalism does not always prize intellectual endeavor, the school compensates by insisting on academic rigor and excellence. It introduces students to both classics of the faith and to literary canons that challenge faith—all in an effort to make them more thoughtful citizens.

Conversations surrounding religion and education, especially in this zone, often fall into a sociological and philosophical orbit. Often this means revisiting the "secularization thesis," which holds that in industrialized, highly educated, and prosperous societies like ours, religion will inevitably and progressively decline. Society will become more and more secularized, and significant people and indeed whole cultures will come to explain the world around them without reference to the sacred, the transcendent, the divine.

If this thesis is true, then religion-related colleges and universities will grow less and less connected to their origins and much less interested in religion and faith. But some people argue that there are too many complicating countersigns for the secularization thesis to survive unquestioned. For too long, one person urged, people have acted as though there were only two education options: utterly secular, "reason-centered" schools on the one hand and narrow, cramped, "faith-based" colleges on the other. But there are many exciting third ways to explore. In the meantime, nostalgia for the old days when churches "ran the show" in higher academia should give way to a creative appraisal of the present landscape.

The liberal arts college is often thought of as a place for preparing students for public life. But there is a way in which the college is *already* a public of its own, or better yet a set of publics. The campus itself includes many such publics: students, faculty, alumni, academic accrediting agencies, local interests, civic groups, and the like. Often these publics conflict with one another. The religious character of a school might impel leaders to work strenuously for harmony among these disparate constituencies. Church-related schools can also excavate their own traditions for resources to address this diversity of publics—and thus exemplify and contribute to public attitudes in other plural contexts far from campus.

What else can church-related institutions of higher education distinctively contribute to academia and the general public? We heard many answers. Such schools provide a special concentration on responsible citizenship. Others emphasize social justice, which does get promoted in critical religious communities but does not erupt spontaneously. Church-related colleges, as they welcome infusions of students and faculty from non-Western countries, provide laboratories for working out questions of intellectual and spiritual diversity. As a school learns more about other cultures and as others observe how they do or do not do this successfully, the result is a deepened global understanding of public religion and its interfaith and intercultural effects.

One participant at a Catholic university with a global perspective emphasized the potential for church-related institutions to take traditions of learning and religion from far and near and relate them to one another. In such efforts, a congenial climate can develop where newcomers make more sense of Western cultures and its religions than they might otherwise have. Meanwhile, Catholic theology commends to American students a global perspective, which foreign students or recent immigrants often bring. Because cultures inevitably clash—over proper gender roles, for instance—in such interactions, the school, its chaplains, and its religion and anthropology professors all have more reason than before to serve as brokers, interpreters, issue sharpeners, and reconcilers. All those efforts add up to the display of public education at a private and religious university.

The Slippery Slope Toward Secularization

Often critics complain that religiously influenced schools have yielded too much to pluralism and secularism. Father James Burtchaell writes in elegiac tones of this problem in Catholic and other religious schools in *The Dying of the Light: The Disengagement of Colleges and Universities from Their Christian Churches*.[1] In lively and honest fashion, Burtchaell chronicles how church-related schools have traveled a slippery slope of adjustments and capitulations down toward secularity.

On the one hand, Burtchaell says that once the Enlightenment faith in science and progress took over the culture, a sense of religious decline in academic institutions was almost inevitable. But on the other hand, he holds many people responsible for the dying of the light: church leaders, college officials, accreditors, status-hungry professors, mentally lazy and unalert or passive alumni, constituents who have either capitulated to secularization or actively sought it. Something might have been done, Burtchaell suggests, to arrest such developments, and some things can still be done to produce at least a few countercultural institutions. Burtchaell envisions as ideal small Catholic colleges, which his critics say would attract few students and be viewed as so eccentric as to dilute their impact on both Catholicism and the wider public.

Burtchaell's Protestant counterpart, George Marsden, brings a Calvinist view to the subject but finds similar trends.[2] Even more than Burtchaell, Marsden sees post-Enlightenment modernism to be the prevailing ethos in higher education. Marsden excoriates some in Christian higher learning who, consciously or not, have sought status and conformity by giving up the "soul" of the university or abandoning the "outrageous" idea of self-consciously Christian scholarship. Marsden's critics say that his models, like Burtchaell's ideal, could not survive in today's competitive collegiate market. Few people—including few conservative Calvinists—would be attracted to such schools. Only a few exceptions could survive, those places where ethnic enclaves, a long history of protection from pluralist impulses, and an extremely dedicated leadership prevail—as at Calvin College in Grand Rapids, Michigan.

Professors Burtchaell and Marsden make some good points, as even their most severe critics admit. Simply observing the current campus scene and noting the many scores of colleges that have drifted from their religious moorings proves that much of their reporting is accurate. Just listen to some faculty and students at church-related colleges as they openly reject the heritages that made their institutions possible. Some of them seem embarrassed to be identified with anything "church-related" in a marketplace they see as secular.

It is true that some faculty at religion-related institutions adopt a "more secular than thou" attitude. They evidently assume that the absence of religious manifestations would somehow enhance the status of their schools. Either they have decided that secularization of all of life's dimensions is inevitable, or they are conformists to a culture that they think values nonreligion. Questions are in order: Have they failed to account for countersecular trends? Are they too transfixed by confining visions of the religious colleges of the past when a new vision is in order?

Also on the scene are those presidents, board members, alumni, constituents, and students who do *not* see a slippery slope toward secularism as an inevitable path. They cannot have and do not want to be part of colleges hermetically sealed from the rest of public life, and they do not want their institutions to rely on and restrict themselves to a homogeneous clientele. For them, being stewards of and participants in life at a church-related university requires an approach that takes its heritage seriously and still welcomes diversity and pluralism, for that context will prepare them well for participating in a public world of differences and yet show them that they can hold on to particular faiths.

Indeed, many private colleges with more moderate or liberal religious connections make a point of salting their student body with exemplars of pluralism. What should we make of a religious school that has an atheist in its philosophy department, or—as at Jesuit-

run Georgetown—a Muslim on its chaplaincy staff? What is sig-
naled if a Lutheran college has a Hindu in its religion department
or if an evangelical college nurtures liberal Protestants on its theology faculty? When college leaders make such decisions and ges-
tures, what is at work? Generosity of spirit? Interfaith risk taking?
Ecumenical tolerance? Catering to multiculturalists? Indifference
to the truth? Are these schools contributing, unwittingly or not, to
the notion that all truths are equal, that all voices deserve an equal
hearing, that all values are relative?

On public campuses, relativism in approaches to knowledge and
truth is understandable. After all, the modern university rarely
embodies more than a very general set of norms, and it has no
mechanism for asserting corporate beliefs in absolutes. But church-
related schools are a different setting, and their supporters may ask,
isn't that a setting where one should be sheltered from relativism?

Church-related colleges may respond that insisting on internal
diversity is one important, structured means of helping students and
faculty engage the world as it really is. Many philosophers and theologians remind us that relativism is by no means a necessary corol-
lary of acknowledging a population's diversity. This strategy must
be carefully executed, of course. But if a church-related college
establishes a climate that encourages broad encounters with often
conflicting materials and ideas, then students and faculty may find
more creative ways to address important issues—even the issue of
relativism itself.

To put this point another way, a church-related college that
intentionally diversifies both student body and faculty can offer
thoughtful approaches to a theology of pluralism. To the degree that
such a theology emerges, it can help people—whether various subpublics or the whole public itself—find their way amid pluralism in
a time when many see relativism as the greatest moral danger.

As church-related colleges encourage students to find and make
spiritual commitments, they can help the public address another

question: How can a diverse public overcome intolerance without weakening strong commitments? Intolerance, as a quick look around our torn and troubled world confirms, can be lethal. But how can citizens overcome this without sliding into what we might call "mere" tolerance? Tolerance can often be a very weak virtue, one not strong enough to structure a vital public arena. Tolerance can often mean simply mutual indifference between people who agree that they don't hold any strong beliefs. Those connected with church-related colleges resist this as they nurture the idea that there are indeed things worth believing very strongly; they cannot settle for a tolerance that is wispy and frail.

The church-related college can serve the public if it can be a scene for the flourishing of what French philosopher Gabriel Marcel called *counterintolerance*.[3] Not shallow, wishy-washy, or simply compromising, counterintolerance comes from someone with deep and profound commitments. But, as Marcel puts it, this person will not use her personal convictions to indict others who hold wrong ideas. Instead, she will use the occasions to examine her own beliefs and the ways she clings to them. Seeing how irreducible and irreplaceable those beliefs are, she can then use this understanding as a means of ensuring that the other person will be received with the same integrity.

If people relate to each other in this way—call it dialogue—this does not rule out conversions. But it does mean that when participants engage in dialogue on church-related college campuses, the issue between them does not take the form of a contest, a winner-take-all battle that seeks to exploit the weaknesses of the other.

Marcel's idea is only one proposal for meeting the challenges of commitment and civility, conviction and diversity. But it holds special promise for people who bring religious and philosophical diversity to church-related institutions of higher education. And this can also be true when dealing with the public beyond the campus. Certainly one can learn counterintolerance in other settings, but church-related colleges provide a public service for those many citizens who look only to such institutions for these kinds of models.

Sustaining academic and religious life on that narrow ridge between relativism and pluralism is certainly precarious. As W. H. Auden put it:

> Perched upon the sharp *arête*,
> Where if we do not move we fall
> Yet movement is heretical
> Since over its ironic rocks
> No route is truly orthodox.[4]

Yet in the minds of those who care about religion and education in our republic, some route must be taken. In the private institutions of higher education with religious roots and ties, this means rethinking what role religion plays in campus life and what role it should play. Those conversations, and the decisions that come from them, will affect the lives of us all.

8

Public Universities
and Graduate Education

S o far, all energies in this book concerning college and university levels have focused on private and church-related institutions, the places where religious inquiry and commitment will be most concentrated and intense. But these represent a small minority of academies. The larger majority are public colleges and universities, which belong to all citizens in each particular place. Public religion poses special challenges and opportunities for these public institutions, so all taxpayers, legislators, trustees, faculty, and students would do well to pay attention.

At first, it may seem futile to ask citizens to be interested in what happens on college and university campuses. After all, only deans and department heads do much to shape the curriculum, and only administrators really influence the allocation of resources. In general, campuses are often quite insulated. The public may hear endlessly about battles over the Western canon, political correctness, Marxist or feminist theory, deconstruction, postmodern relativism, or the salary of the football coach, but it can often do little more than react. How would taxpayers influence or interfere in such matters?

Although opportunities for involvement may be limited, it is still vitally important for citizens of all kinds to care about what goes on in public institutions of higher education. Given their influence over the whole of culture and society, universities need to be observed, analyzed, and monitored. And what universities discover, teach, and practice reveals far too much about the larger society for citizens to neglect what goes on there. Because they insist on academic freedom, university faculty and students may be constantly testing the boundaries of the permissible and the thinkable. But over the long run, institutions must respond to the wider public, which pays the bills, and this can make universities important barometers of public opinion.

To continue the meteorological metaphor: institutions of higher education may represent the intellectual winds that blow, the moral storms that break out, the spiritual solar energy devices that redirect forces that directly affect the citizenry. Anyone alive and alert during the 1960s need not be reminded of the influence that campus dissent, protest, and reaction can have on foreign policy, race relations, or lifestyle options. Though the influence may seem more subtle today, it is no less pervasive.

A Range of Options: Educational Leaders and Choice About Religion

University attitudes about religion bear on both curriculum and pedagogy, and these in turn bear on religion in the public arena. If educators are hostile to religion in all its forms, or if they merely ignore it, this can affect society's sense of whether religion is an important element of civic life. If a state-supported institution does make room for religion but only in a small, isolated department of religious studies, it has indicated that religion has definable limits and should be kept in its box.

A university may make room for religion, of course, without drawing resources together in a single department. Advocates of a more broad-based approach to religion may argue that religion already suffuses many areas of study and it is in these different contexts that religion is best understood. Cultural anthropologists, area studies specialists, psychologists, sociologists, philosophers, and lit-erary critics, among others, can all touch on religion in their work. When educational leaders argue for this position, they thereby indi-cate that religion, though important, lacks precise definition and limits.

Other options are also available. A university may characteristi-cally engage in nothing but critical dismissal of religion, and this has social consequences. If faculty unite in their belief that religious faith can be reduced to other things—human projection, illusion, misap-plied belief—that posture may influence the outlooks of both students and the wider society. Also, if an institution of higher education con-sciously fails to reflect the religious realities of the world around it, it may be dismissed as out of touch, out of range, an ivory tower.

This array of options for public universities holds true, generally speaking, for the options available to their privately run counterparts, especially when it comes to graduate education. There are significant differences among such schools, naturally. For example, Harvard, Yale, Chicago, Notre Dame, Vanderbilt, and others with historical denom-inational ties such as Emory and Southern Methodist can without controversy host divinity schools and graduate theological schools and help prepare religious professionals for their vocations. State uni-versities, by contrast, might study religion, but they won't dabble in practical ministerial education. Further, although places such as Florida State or the University of California, Santa Barbara, may house very large, productive, and well-regarded departments of reli-gious studies, their faculties will be especially mindful to resist con-fessional or "insider" perspectives in their teaching.

Differentiating Public and Private Schools with Respect to Religion

Distinguishing between private and public institutions of higher education means little in practice. Although in the religious stud-ies programs of private universities there are no taxpayer interests to keep in mind, the academic ethos dictates that all university teaching proceed on a single track with respect to creeds and commitments. If one looks for subtleties, perhaps it is true that private institutions have an easier time supporting departments of theology. If theology means the interpretation of the life of a people in light of a transcendent reference, it implies an insider character. Public universities are usually wary of doing theology, whether Jewish, Christian, Muslim, feminist, or African American, to name several options. Public institutions will teach theology historically, philosophically, phenomenologically—as private schools also often do—but they will be reluctant to teach from a particular religious perspective.

This is not to suggest that classrooms in private institutions, even in divinity and theological schools, are turned into places for worship or evangelism. The vast majority of professors have been conditioned by graduate school and life in a pluralist society to be cautious about the language they use in different settings. They are mindful of an implicit covenant with students who hold a variety of worldviews, a responsibility not to violate the pedagogical boundaries with proselytizing.

Some critics of higher education complain that professors have been too conditioned toward metaphysical neutrality by their graduate education. They have become too unready to be judgmental, prophetic, hortatory, or evangelistic. Instead of tenured professors thinking of themselves as, paradoxically or oxymoronically, "resident aliens" in academic culture, they are instead too sufficiently at home, not alien enough, unready to break free of convention. Whether or not this is fair, the fact that such criticism is heard suggests that a similar, special ethos does tend to pervade all public and much private university education.

Because of this similarity, we will henceforth not make as much of a point of distinctions such as "public" or "private," "graduate" or "professional," and will simply use the word *university* to refer to the highest-level research, inquiry, teaching, and transmission.

The Public Institution and Its Environment

Universities, in addition to reflecting the auspices under which they educate, also tend to be strongly influenced by their environment, even if sometimes by countering it. For example, the University of Wisconsin at Madison thrives in a state that enjoys high levels of church participation and attendance. Yet as part of its mission, the school has for decades also welcomed critics of religion and discouraged graduate-level teaching that involves religion close to home. In such places, one could until recently pursue a doctorate in Buddhist or Hindu studies, justified in part because of the assumption that Asian cultures cannot be understood without some knowledge of Asian religions. But the university made no room, except incidentally, for graduate work on Judaism, Catholicism, or Protestantism. Behind this is the unexamined assumption that North American cultures *can* be understood without reckoning with the role of religion, or at least that such knowledge can be gained without a concentrated, separate endeavor dealing with religion as a subject in itself.

In such places, observers who are nervous about public religion invoke the "separation of church and state." Other state universities have laws and codes that in effect construct thick barriers against the intrusion of religion on academic matters. Thus Washington, a state that differs vastly from Wisconsin in terms of citizen participation in religious institutions, has laws that keep religion at a safe distance in its various state universities.

I am not trying to make the case that religion is completely absent, effectively screened out, and receives no encouragement in such settings. Many faculty treat the subject of religion generally while covering their disciplines. What does not appear, however, is a department, a field, an area, a concentration, a place where faculty and students can sustain collegial and mutual discovery across generations.

By contrast, state universities elsewhere may more directly reflect the religious expectations and ethos of a particular region. Thus Utah State reflects a Mormon environment, and leaders at the University of Alabama know they inhabit the center of Baptist culture. All one needs to do is read the bulletin boards and watch students pour into campus religious centers to realize the religious character of these educational environments. In such places, "public religion" has a different meaning than in places characterized by true religious pluralism. An art student who wants to flaunt local conventions will not waste time offending Mormons if attending the University of Maine or creating work that scandalizes Catholic sensibilities if a student at the University of Mississippi. Artistic Molotov cocktails can be effective only if the walls of the Vatican or the Mormon Temple are, culturally speaking, within range.

Most private universities, beginning with Harvard, Yale, Brown, and Princeton, originated as expressions of church communities. Some reflected their genesis and genius more consistently than others. Well into the twentieth century, Princeton remained a place where faculty could push the boundaries of Presbyterianism only with great difficulty. Today, the Scottish commonsense realism that remained in favor through the presidency of alumnus Woodrow Wilson would not be taught at the university proper but relegated to the nearby Princeton Theological Seminary—and it is not likely that it would show up even there.

Why Universities Turned Ever More Secular

For the most part, private schools moved from their theological and ecclesiastical roots. And those institutions that had a later start, such as Johns Hopkins or Cornell, excluded from the beginning most formal study of religion. (Some places, such as Cornell, then compensated for this exclusion by constructing elaborate worship spaces or prominent chapels.) As modern graduate education developed, pioneers often used German paradigms and certain models of modernity. This resulted in more specialization in university study, and religion was moved to the margins, almost always intellectually and sometimes physically. Theological schools were sometimes exiled from the main campus and forced to do their own fundraising. Many disciplinary pioneers came to find their beginnings in village pietism confining. John Dewey, for example, spoke of the "inward laceration" of his childhood New England Congregationalist culture,[1] and others indicated a similar desire to be liberated from these early religious experiences. There is no question that over time and for many reasons, religious inquiry diminished as a presence in higher education.

Why Religion Returned to Universities

Universities did not all become aggressively or even reflexively secularistic. Around the middle of the twentieth century, religious studies began to make a surprising and organized return to higher education. White Protestants still dominated the culture and the academy then, and many leaders, shocked by the moral chaos and antidemocratic sentiments manifested in World War II, argued that universities must reexplore religion. For them, this meant the religious traditions of the West, religion in general, religion as a moral motivator, and especially the humanistic values associated with Christian and then "Judeo-Christian" experience. Some of these pioneers, located at Princeton, Harvard, Yale, and Chicago, undertook to introduce or reintroduce religion formally into the curriculum at trailblazing institutions such as the University of Iowa. Others followed. In the course of half a century, tax-supported universities with visible religious studies programs increased from a handful to more than nine hundred.

Other forces contributed to this increase, again reflecting the public interest and public religion. For example, ex-GIs, children of the Depression influenced by what they saw in the Second World War, settled down with spouses and families on campuses and created a climate conducive to religious participation. The GI Bill, designed to compensate soldiers for years lost from college, subsidized the education of millions who had grown up in contexts where religion had been naturally integrated into their lives. They had no problem with that influence continuing in campus life; in fact, they even welcomed it. Before the GI Bill, only a small percentage of Catholics attended universities, but in the following decades, Catholics became one of the most highly university-educated groups. Many Catholics attended public universities and were more ready than others to see religion treated well by administrators and faculty. Campus ministries prospered throughout the 1950s, and chapels and religious centers arose.

Another force had a great deal of influence. After the Soviet Union launched *Sputnik* in 1957, a new technological phase in the Cold War led American universities to advertise themselves as the places where research for "our side" of the space race would occur. As universities found it easier than before to gain funds and expand, the humanities got a relatively free ride. Among them, teachers in disciplines such as "comparative religion" (as the government liked to speak of it) were poised to take advantage of this opening. Advocates of this approach found a home in most major universities.

Still another factor was the increasing curiosity about spiritual life engendered by the cultural shifts of the 1960s. In some places, religion, with its prophetic edge, resonated with activists for racial equality and against the Vietnam War. Chapels often became the nerve centers of nonviolent protests. The classroom offered the chance to study the religious texts that once inspired people to revolt and that might inspire and guide them again.

As that activism subsided, many students began to satisfy that quickened religious interest by turning toward more exotic and esoteric religions. By the 1970s, university bulletin boards advertised innumerable curricular options for spiritual seekers. Where better to learn about witches, vision-inducing drugs, and alternative spiritual options than in the religious studies departments, with courses on Zen and the occult? Some of these energies trickled upward along the paths of curiosity and resulted in formal curricular changes.

This is not the place to write a cultural history of the postwar twentieth century beyond noting the many reasons why universities have become more hospitable to the study and expression of religion in public life. Emphatically, this turn did not reach all parts of all universities equally. In many places, a secular ethos still pervades institutions of higher education. Religion, as its curricular champions make clear, still tends to be underfunded and underappreciated— whatever "full appreciation" might entail. These days, the study of religion prospers or declines along with the humanities in general.

Barriers to Fuller Expression of Religion

As a latecomer to the departmental scene, religion often sees its fortunes rise and fall with those of the humanities, and when the fiscal pinch is severe, religion especially suffers. In other words, changing faculty attitudes toward religion and religious understandings did not mean that academics developed a wholesale fundamental openness to the subject. There was no simple shift away from the "secular only" attitude that had been taken for granted in higher education.

Often these conflicts occur between philosophy and religion scholars. In part, this happens because these two faculties seem to be working some of the same territory. In many schools, the upstart religionists drew more students to their classes than most philosophers did. Religious scholars often seemed to be more alert to the needs and curiosities of contemporary students than professors in cognate disciplines.

Policy difficulties developed along the way. A perceptual gap existed between the "real world" and many academics' understanding of what was real. Where religion had been previously misrepresented and misunderstood, the increased religious presence on campus led to mistrust—and often with good reason. Some observers worried about the separation of church and state. Though court rulings usually dealt with religion and education at the lower educational levels, many critics used the wall metaphor to make the case for excluding religion from higher education.

A Day with a University Board and What It Revealed

I experienced a sample of this at a major midwestern state university, where I was to make a case for including religious studies. In a previous meeting, one trustee, with an admirable record on civil rights, had questioned whether religion had played a sufficiently significant role in human affairs to take up time at a university. He knew that his state contained many churches, which attracted sizable congregations. But in the trustee's eyes, what religious people busied themselves with had mostly to do with weekends and leisure time, residential and family life. Of course, he knew that universities should care about such things, but only in a casual way. What really mattered in his world were government and politics, business and commerce, economics and political science, resource allocation, agricultural policies, urban issues. Where did religion fit in with respect to those weighty matters? The implicit answer was—nowhere. So keep religious studies out of the university.

It so happened that on the train that day, I had red-penciled my way through the *New York Times*. A Buddhist monk had immolated himself in front of the United Nations. Religious controversy had entered a New York mayoral campaign. Even ruling out many implicit and disguised appearances, there were eighteen important stories that day in which religion was an explicit theme. All of the references concerned life outside the sanctuary, at the crossroads to which the trustee had referred.

After this parable countering the notion that religion is trivial, we should say two things. First, life *in* the sanctuary is also of public importance. Half the American people gather quite regularly to listen, pray, and organize their weeks in the light of what they understand as God's word. The sermons and sacraments, the bar mitzvahs and confirmations, the songs and prayer, the Sabbath or Sunday bulletins, all signal what religious people find important. What happens in the sanctuary colors how people view the world, human rights, national policies, war and peace, allocation of resources, and health care. When scholars of religion study the response to myth and symbols, rites and ceremonies, they are not examining a merely private world with only private meanings.

The other thing that needs saying is that my Midwest campus story, now three or four decades old, occurred at a time when religion's public role was more disguised than it is in the new century. Yes, there was a boom in church construction to house newly suburbanized Christians and Jews. African Americans, many from the rural South, and Hispanic immigrants were moving into inner cities and revitalizing churches, remodeling old religious structures, and filling storefronts with worship in unprecedented ways. Religion was "all over the place" in institutional forms.

Religion had not gone into hiding, even physically or structurally. President Eisenhower had made religion a vivid presence in his White House and his programs, which he called his Crusade. Senator John F. Kennedy's Catholicism had inspired national debate. Billy Graham crusaded; Fulton Sheen was on TV; Rabbi Abraham Joshua Heschel witnessed to the presence of God in classrooms and civil rights struggles. But unlike today, when journalists often have to deal with religion in front-page matters, the press still tended to restrict religion to a half page "above the ads" in Saturday's newspaper.

With these two observations made, we return to the scene before the university's board of trustees. The trustees agreed that the eighteen newspaper stories did indeed merit attention. Then I started asking them questions. How does one judge the Buddhist monk without knowing what Buddhism or a monk actually is? How can the public begin to determine whether his act was aberrant or religiously sanctioned without understanding his religious context? How could collegians intelligently assess how his act might play in Christian churches, where martyrdom is celebrated throughout the church year? Would the monk's act only further divide hawks and doves, who both make moral cases on religious grounds? A sigh of relief was audible when we turned our attention to the tamer, more familiar matter of religion in the New York mayoral race. But there were still sixteen other stories to go.

We won some; we lost some; but the day was a winner for the cause. The university voted to abolish dated, inadequate, and weak ways of addressing religion to make room for the serious study of its influence. In the ensuing years, something similar occurred on hundreds of campuses.

Church-State Issues

As religious studies carved out a place in the curriculum and on campus, many new issues emerged concerning church and state. Some became the focus of litigation, as in the case of *Rosenberger* v. *University of Virginia* (1995), where the Supreme Court ruled that an evangelical Christian group deserved equal access with other campus groups to student-provided activity funds. At Yale, some Orthodox Jewish students sued because they did not want to live in mixed-gender dormitories. The future promises similar cases dealing with religion in the context of higher education.

However, as far as curriculum and classroom are concerned, anxieties about violating church-state boundaries have turned out to be almost completely unfounded. Of course, believers who describe themselves as critical and prophetic might say that's the problem exactly. Why don't we hear more criticism of or litigation against university instructors for religious reasons? Do they too readily accept the secular mores of higher education? Should they not be acting prophetically, trying to topple the assumptions by which the university is erroneously run? Such questions are important, but they need not distract us from our agenda of addressing larger questions about religion and higher education.

9

Religion and Higher Education

A Specific Agenda for Advancing the Conversation

No one can predict with certainty what is in store for the humanities and especially for religion in the humanities. But looking ahead, we see many important issues that must be addressed in advancing a conversation on religion and higher education. By eavesdropping on conversations we held at the Public Religion Project, we hope that certain trajectories emerge that can frame future conversations in many communities, including yours. So pull up a figurative chair and listen in with us as experts, scholars, and other concerned citizens survey the field and highlight important questions, all of which have inescapable and significant public ramifications.

Critical Questions for Education and Religion

Can American life really be understood without religion? Several years ago, a Chinese university scholar on study leave knocked on my door and starting showing up in classes. He told me that more and more Chinese historians of American life found that they could not tell the American story without referring to the religion that was webbed into it. Yet they had to do so indirectly, inventing terms that helped them avoid the term *religion* and job descriptions that kept them from being described as "experts on religion." They could not, however, avoid that religious web if they wanted to deal intelligently with America. If from the distance of China, scholars insist that the spiritual dimension is essential to the American story, those at closer range ignore religion in America at their intellectual peril.

Should universities consider student interests when determining what subjects are important? Thirty-five years ago, a university leader, newly alert to the role of religion in the civil rights movement, began to study it at the level of higher education. This leader proposed that educators survey student interests each year to obtain a more accurate picture of their experiences and curiosities. Thus in recent decades, noted this scholar, students have pushed forward and emphasized spiritual themes, and many have undergone spiritual searches.

Clearly, an academic institution does *not* have to play the role of corporate guru, shaman, priest, or counselor; indeed, it would probably perform these roles poorly if it tried. A university is not a shrine, a temple, an altar, or a church. But anyone who studies history and other parts of the humanities knows that the spiritual interests of the students reflect widespread, if not universal, impulses.

Students voice these sentiments and report on their experiences, thus creating raw material that deserves study. Faculty members are too often caught off guard, unable to address their students' intellectual and spiritual agendas. Many professors were trained in times and places that slighted or discouraged such concerns. But any whining about the past should give way to preparing for a different future. On almost every subject, religion may and should arise, and higher education best serves its students by being ready to tackle religious concerns.

Should universities accept more than one approach to religion? If religion continues to hold its place in the university curriculum, is it appropriate, asks a person of faith, that all religious inquiry be reduced to a single approach? Heads often turn when someone suggests that a single approach prevails in the academy, as diverse as universities and faculties are. But one conversation participant claimed that this great methodological variety only disguises a deeper reality: that academic approaches to religion conform to a certain pattern of Western philosophical rationalism and scientific skepticism.

This means that while teachers may be privately religious, they will disguise this and try to appear disinterested in the public of the classroom situation. Then the question arises, if many faculty reason without a transcendent frame of reference, why is it so outlandish to make room for individuals whose worldviews are anchored by God? Would not the university be well served by representing more points of view?

Through the ages, learning has included religious inquiry based on religious commitment. Did the eighteenth-century Enlightenment and its modernist successors unhistorically wipe out this record? Shouldn't universities be more metaphysically pluralist than they have been? Many university campuses house scholarly institutes devoted to the study of religion. Doesn't this indicate that students are unfairly kept from pursuing such interests within the boundaries of the regular classroom? Has anyone noticed that such institutes usually have more impact on public policy than on their university hosts?

Should the religious element in higher education reflect contemporary issues? From another state university leader came this well-posed question: Should a university simply reflect its surrounding culture, or should it try to transcend its environment in important aspects? When technocorporate interests dominate, should universities be concerned with little else than funneling students into those careers? Why assume that higher education must adapt to the surrounding culture, as though that culture is complete, satisfying, fulfilled and fulfilling, the climax of human endeavor? Should universities play a part in examining and questioning a culture's assumptions?

The same participant also raised questions about what happens when religious studies is *too* successful, too attractive. Most listeners chuckled, unable to picture such a thing happening, but there are reasons to be alert on this front. In some schools, the administration wants to establish doctoral programs in this field in order to promote its own reputation as a well-rounded institution—even though there is and will likely remain a glut of Ph.D.'s for some time to come. This issue clearly has public consequences. How should academic societies and the wider public address it?

Should universities treat religion as a separate subject? Some of our conversation participants contended that the field of religious studies has made its way by coasting along and profiting from the relative prosperity of other disciplines. It seems to depend on anthropology, sociology, psychology, history, philosophy, and literature. Should religious studies hitchhike on these other disciplines? If religion indeed has public consequences, should not the field of religious studies stand on its own? Isn't there something distinctive about the subject and methods of religious studies?

At first glance, this enduring topic seems to be less relevant to the issue of public religion and education, given that the public—and who can blame it?—evinces little interest in methodological questions. But scholars must debate such issues if religious studies is to secure a place in higher education. If everything can be accomplished in other departments and disciplines, the case for a comprehensive curricular approach to religion seems more shaky.

Is religion waxing or waning as a social force? Many conversation partners complained that people in public institutions hold a "declinist" view of religion. If religion is disappearing, as declinists contend, why bother to study it, make a place for it, or understand it? Why not save all such vanishing subjects for the history and archaeology departments?

Such a view, according to our participants, is narrow, partial, and limited to what one can see out the windows of Western Europe and North America. When universities slight religion, this means that they are operating in isolation from local manifestations of the subject matter. When they study even their own pluralist environment, including the various endeavors of local religious groups and individuals, students become better informed about the world in which they soon will live. The public sphere, students should learn, is home not only to conservative "Christian coalitions" or faraway ethnoreligious conflicts but also to a more complex local scene that merits further study.

Why do university students disdain mainstream faiths in favor of other alternatives? A liberal arts professor described his institution. Founded by post-Puritan pastors but having abandoned its roots, this school now finds religious practice vital only among some Catholics and Jews. (There are few visible evangelical gatherings in his part of the country.) And mainstream Protestantism, the school's ancestry and long the main standard-bearer for religion in the academy, attracts little notice. Tibetan Buddhism seems closer and more relevant to students than local churches.

Religious studies on campus is prized, but this is the case more for studying non-Christian phenomena. Yet when one seriously studies the Western classics and attracts students, they find it intellectually challenging. It is appropriate, we heard, to ask how long university students will continue to shrug off the Catholicism or Protestantism that is "right at home" in favor of studying more distant and esoteric religions. What does this hunger for the exotic mean for the public and public religion among such student elites?

How do universities relate to increasingly complex religious practices? A university chaplain noted that when assessing her campus, religiously speaking, *transformation* is the watchword. Students bring spiritual questions and in many ways become more at ease than before in "going public" with their searches. But most remain uninterested in organized religion, which for them means the kind of self-seeking and boring institutions they remember from their hometowns.

Some students do come closer to their religious inheritance when they explore ethics. In medical ethics and similar fields, students often find that addressing the deepest and most troubling life issues means that theological norms have to become part of the discussion. We heard the story of one faculty member who, in a speech addressing an incoming class, crowed proudly about the amorality of the university and of universities, contending that such institutions are amoral by design, ideology, and practice. Many students reacted negatively, responding that universities unsystematically teach morals all the time. When responding to such instruction, students often discover that discussions soon take on an unavoidable religious and philosophical cast.

How do instructors integrate particular religious viewpoints into the study of religion? Another teacher at a major private university is clearly identified with a particular religious tradition and has written scholarly books with a tinge of insider vision about them. But this does not come up in his teaching. He knows from personal experience that religion has much to do with the practice of living. Is the university the proper place to employ religious insights to ask questions of truth? One may believe in divine truth, but how does this get put into operation in history and other disciplines? Do religious questions of truth fall outside the university's boundaries?

Can the modern university ever be a hospitable place for pursuing religious faith? Against the general celebration of the public manifestations of religion in higher education, a dissenter enlivened our conversation by wondering whether religious leaders have been too eager to be accepted by, and acceptable to, the public. Perhaps, our dissenter suggested, this desire has come at the expense of anything resembling true religious passion and conviction.

We sought analogues. On the elementary level, some home schoolers think that their example and intention will have public consequences. They ask, as one of our conversation partners did, if it might not make the most sense to abandon public education as a lost cause and instead support religiously based alternatives. There is more than one way for believing people to relate to the culture around them. Perhaps only religion taught "from within" can maintain spiritual integrity; in the public university, certain spiritual aspects may be compromised.

Can Americans still be drawn together by some common narrative? A theologian noted that professors of religion often avoid theological questions, even those that merit attention and come up in unexpected but appropriate places. Often such questions are avoided by asserting the deconstructive or postmodern claim that there are no assured, stable meanings in texts, including sacred texts. The only truth is situated truth, not unified and objective truth, which means that there can be no "grand narrative," whether of God's relationship to humanity, divine presence in religious community, or theological meanings in the unfolding American experience.

Perhaps the grand narrative, rooted in scripture and culturally central, is rightfully in trouble today, for it has often been exclusive and narrow. But an ever more complex America both needs and generates elements of a more complex narrative, and this story has and will have religious dimensions. This transformation, if well observed, could provide a foundation for interpreting public life today. To face that prospect and address it creatively is more valuable than to imitate fashionable and passing theories.

Does America's spiritual diversity doom the impartial study of religion? A professor and administrator focused on several problems internal to universities. As interest in religion expands, scholars from other fields often know too little about the subject to inform the debate. A common religious vocabulary seems beyond reach, and even the aspiration to develop one has atrophied or fallen out of fashion. It would be foolish not to acknowledge the pluralism in American public life, but an acceptance of the country's "manyness" has kept many scholars from efforts to move beyond the boundaries of particular communities. Finally, much of the religion at universities is disconnected from how people actually live. When the public hears at all about what universities say about religion, it probably sounds more like interoffice memoranda than anything else. More attention to the public agenda can improve curricula and teaching.

How do foreigners perceive the role of religious faith in America? A specialist in world religions told us that students from other parts of the globe are mystified by the sense that universities favor talk about spirituality over religion. They are puzzled that students would rather study remote expressions of faith than those closer to home. They have trouble with faculty and students who seem unable to appreciate the cultural place and power of religious institutions, especially given the obvious role such institutions have played in their own countries' histories. While churches in Africa encourage better resource management and lead a "green revolution," visitors perceive more affluent American churches as less instrumental in such causes. Yet these institutions play major roles in the voluntary sector, and they deserve study.

The overseas guests see how religious agencies in their cultures patronize the arts. Why is there not a similar stimulation of creativity in this country? How should the churches and others collaborate? Perhaps Americans have convinced themselves so thoroughly that religious studies is a humanistic end in itself that they overlook the ways religion changes lives, sparks wars, and serves to reconcile. Couldn't religion's better causes be furthered by universities? It is urgent, we heard, to develop new models for the way religion intersects with public interests. It may be that newly fashioned institutes (such as those at Harvard, Princeton, and Chicago) might advance some of this work before the curriculum addresses it.

Can the university guarantee religious questions that would serve as effective cultural criticism? A chaplain spoke up about the prophetic role of religion. With others, he has witnessed the disorientation of many students as they are oriented toward the market and consumer corporate culture. Students will participate in that culture, whether they like it or not. Does the university provide them with the critical tools to search for constructive alternatives? Can they find and use these without touching on religious questions?

Can religious studies enliven the humanities and focus universitywide inquiries? A veteran in religious studies work and methodologies found that pursuing religious studies is a creative way to expose the frequently noted absence of authority, leadership, and creativity at the administrative level. In the humanities, most schools seem to be bereft of clear statements of mission and intention. In one telling incident, faculty members wanted to use university resources to probe the ethical use of animals in medical research. University leaders did not know where to place such research, so they handed the responsibility to the part of the university working on the Human Genome Project. Have universities accurate maps of the humanities to match the real world of today? Can religion help sketch such maps?

Should the university recognize and coordinate the transcultural elements in religious studies? A humanities dean was congratulatory and hopeful. This person admitted to overworking professors in religious studies because, for all their specialization, their discipline attaches itself to so many human interests and concerns. They can move laterally. Something in their preparation tends to equip all those who forgo intense specialization with broader humanistic sensibilities. Religious studies is a place where faculty are less bound by a single time, place, culture, or subject matter. That makes religious studies difficult, but it can also be a model for more parts of the university as it tries to assume public roles on vital issues.

Should universities enable students to critique religious traditions? A teacher of Christian history believes the university is a place where attitudes toward religion can develop in ways that are good for public understandings. Often students who come from a particular background—Jewish, Muslim, Episcopal, or whatever— think that they already understand the content and practices of that religion. This causes them to underestimate a tradition's potential, for good or evil. University-level study can help inform and refine perceptions of the various religious traditions that make up public life.

What motivates religious studies in a time of cultural crisis? Has all this been too luxurious a conversation? Did the Public Religion Project talk and talk while the world around it threatened to self-destruct? One scholar, a specialist in the history of higher education and the place of religious studies within it, stressed how important it is to see what became of original intentions. At one time, the motive behind religious studies was to help ensure the understanding of a civilization and to come up with ways to promote national and international morality. Today, religious studies is more given to the disinterested study of religion, at least rhetorically speaking. There are, of course, self-conscious exceptions to this in disciplines that forthrightly analyze the negative and positive elements of religion in public affairs.

What worldviews are held by scholars and students who study religion? The students of a sociologist of religion ask, when is religious faith made explicit in academic inquiry? Faculties usually shy away from this natural question. How conscious are faculty that they reveal implicit commitments all the time? Students want to know why professors remain wary of discussing close-to-home religion. Even though this sociologist's state university welcomes endowments for the study of Buddhism and Hinduism, the institution would be very nervous about a Catholic chair or an institute for studying evangelicalism—even though around half of all Americans identify with these two religious groups.

With this observation came a range of questions. Why the nervousness? What can we learn from answers to that question? Why is religious experience noted everywhere but in the classroom? Can one understand a phenomenon without giving weight to the experience and expression of it? Students are more ready than faculty for the personal dimension. Do professors feel restrained lest they upset the pluralist mix, while those in the pluralist mix are ready for more open and forthright discussions of religious issues?

Should universities pursue "real life" religious issues on campus? One religion scholar urges colleagues not to reduce and confine the subject of religion and higher education too readily. Even in the spheres of undergraduate religious studies, graduate studies, and the divinity school where this professor teaches, there is room for vastly different questions and approaches. What is needed next is a careful mapping of university studies, with an eye toward what these different campus contexts represent as examples of public concerns. Having taught at first a public and now a private university, this scholar urged more examination of the differences between the arenas. Have faculty spent too much time working on lesser problems, such as research protocols, while major problems affect the personal level? Universities seek to know what religions have to say on issues such as same-sex unions, gender roles, homosexuality, and violence. Students look for faculty to model how to engage these issues; they bring much to the encounter themselves. Are faculty properly trained and ready to give back?

What is the proper relationship between religious commitment and higher education? A senior scholar at a private university saw the public role of religion denatured at schools where questions of truth are bracketed or even dismissed. Do religions make sense unless those claims get represented and addressed?

The public knows what to make of the knowledge professed by religious preachers and counselors, but it often has trouble understanding the point of noncommittal, abstract, and distant study of religion. If the larger narratives that infuse both religion and public life are disappearing, what will take their place? Often institutions of higher education and their faculties think they can stay on the sidelines and watch the culture's stories and meanings be transacted apart from the academy. Then they turn around and criticize the cultural products. Instead of coming in at the end of the game, universities could play a constructive role by contributing to the development and analysis of these new narratives.

A Caveat About Cultural Attentiveness

After making the case for cultural alertness, a caveat is in order. Higher education cannot be set up to respond to any particular cultural moment or what the present market demands. This is especially true in the case of religion and religious studies. Although religion has a reputation for being very conservative and traditional, in a competitive and market-oriented nation there will always be "supply side" religious leaders who try to satisfy new cultural tastes and interests. Such leaders will peddle their wares and in this or other ways influence the agenda of universities.

Thus in the mid-1990s, a university could have created an attractive set of courses on angels; no doubt many did. New Age spiritualists and adventurous church members united in supporting television programs about angels. The public purchased plastic cherubs and made best-sellers of various angel books.

But two years later, the passion for angels waned. Instead, for a year or two, observers noted an intense interest in near-death experiences, tales of "the other side," and communicating with the dead. However, before curricula fully adjusted to this latest cultural trend, the millennium loomed. A perfectly legitimate topic for some courses, millennial writing could not sustain itself long after the turn of the century. Tailoring a curriculum to meet changing tastes, shaped by the media and consumer culture as they are, would be unwise. Being attentive to cultural interests is not the same as windsocking with every cultural breeze.

Two Kinds of Relevance: Intrinsic and Imposed

One helpful distinction to make comes from Alfred Schutz.[1] He writes in difficult terms, translated here into simpler form, of some foci of consciousness and intention as being marked by *intrinsic relevance*. These represent enduring issues, concerns that do not come and go. Most specialists pursue some field or other for its intrinsic relevance. The chemist does not have to justify each day whatever prompts her to enter the laboratory for basic research. This historian may select topics because they quicken his curiosity but that seem to have few immediate connections to the surrounding world.

Imposed relevance is the other kind of attraction, according to Schutz. The United States entered the Vietnam conflict with only a handful of experts who knew anything about the language, traditions, and religion of the area's allies and enemies. A lethal situation soon arose. The war "imposed" the relevance of Southeast Asian studies on the American population.

In the best of circumstances, the two kinds of relevance inter-sect and overlap. Scholars tend to cover a wide range of issues, pur-suing them as if for their own sake, and then something in the environment evokes their carefully acquired expertise. These two kinds of relevance can help illuminate the present theme. The ini-tial lack of interest in university-level religious studies produced a situation in which, it can be argued, the academy was not suffi-ciently monitoring, assessing, informing, or disseminating informa-tion about religion. The university has been involved in catch-up work on this front ever since. And although religious studies has established itself, it cannot be said that the academy at large is as yet completely at home with religion. It is caught off guard when situations of imposed relevance occur.

Thinking in terms of these two kinds of relevance, intrinsic and imposed, helps educational leaders and citizens at large become aware of the limits to higher education's charter and competence. Some critics fault universities for not promoting religion more overtly, but the public university is not and cannot become a nurs-ery of faith, an agency of regular worship, a place where in compen-sation for past neglect religion is given disproportionate emphasis. (I hesitate to insert a note: by including that last line, I have not lost all touch with reality. There is no danger that religion will be over-stressed on public university campuses in the present climate, espe-cially given the unfolding situation of American pluralism. But we must examine all the tendencies and contingencies when working to discuss a proper place for the forces of faith and spirituality.)

Inevitably, individual scholars provide examples and colorations of this subject in their work all along. The atheist who comments on intensified Hindu-Christian conflict in India may well dismiss it with, "Oh, that's how religious people always are." Another may teach about Hindu-Muslim India and instead focus on Mother Teresa, commending her minority Catholic faith there while doing so. Those are extremes. But universities as a whole have no consistent way of coordinating the pro and con dimensions of religious inquiry and discovery. They have enough to do without becoming anything like churches and temples of their own.

Universities are not designed, called, or equipped to appraise all the faiths around them disinterestedly. Many of them do fair-minded teaching about what other faiths represent. Many church or synagogue classes do in fact take tours to see the worship, architecture, and outreach of other bodies, but they do this occasionally, casually, and incidentally to their other work and tend to appraise what they see and experience through the interpreting eyes of their own faith community.

Agencies of government certainly have no mission to do such comprehending of reality. If they tried, they would soon be in the business of defining and in effect legitimating and licensing some expressions of faith and demeaning or penalizing those they do not favor. Private industry is not motivated or poised to do anything of this sort. The nearest competitors for fulfilling this assignment are the church-related institutions of higher education. They may do this study effectively and fair-mindedly. But the resources for the task are limited, and there will always be suspicion that the studies will be biased. In any case, more perspectives than their own should be welcomed.

So we are left with universities, which both by definition and accident in a liberal culture will reflect the ethos of all or parts of society. Emphatically: that outlook and set of practices of the universities need not, does not, and should not square with the message and intention of many religious groups. Tax-supported academies will continue to favor skeptical rationality as their main mode of inquiry, thus biasing it in one way. Religious groups may also make room for the skeptic and the inquirer, but their essential task is to promote faith, which may mean that they call for at least temporary or partial shelving of the only-skeptical approach, thus biasing inquiry in a different way.

Universities are to teach tolerance and to be indifferent to the truth claims of any particular faith. Yet particular believers, though they can be tolerant, cannot be indifferent. Universities go with the flow of the culture and put their accent on individual expression. Yet religious groups are groups, which means they stimulate community life in ways that may at least partly contradict the norms of the academy and the larger culture.

Without skeptical rationality as the norm, tolerance as the goal, and individualism as an instinctive assumption, Western universities would not exist or would be too corrupted to be of positive use. Yet religious forces and leaders know that those three elements in isolation could be corrosive of faith and would hamper the attention to loyalty and commitment to religious communities. So the available collection of approaches to study and inquiry about religion and the available collection of approaches to the practices of and worship in religion as expressed in communities can live in often tense but therefore quite creative interplay.

When the task of religious study centers on a description of life, rather than a prescription for life, one is not to pursue it in the chapel or the sanctuary. It belongs in the classroom, library, and laboratory. Meanwhile, the chapel whose leaders are content with description alone will have failed its own congregants. The people who sign up for and are loyal to religious institutions might enjoy hearing that some scientists, philosophers, and other setters of the intellectual pace are believers. But most of these people would be the last to want the priests to become professors of public theology. People do not want religious leaders to be leaders of worship by the general public in a mood of prayer "to whom it may concern." People may want these leaders to be tolerant but also expect focus and commitment. So professor and priest have separate callings in a society that needs the distinctive specialized skills of both.

10

After Listening, a Time to Act

Whoever has paid attention to recent academic and cultural debates can see that I have been sensitive to the question of "the public." Many culture critics do not even think there is such as thing as "the public" or that it is fair to talk about "the public." In this book, we have not avoided talking about "the public." But we should probably spend some time tidying the issue.

With respect to religion, how should "the public" be served by its schools? How can private and church-related colleges serve "the public"? And how can public universities regard and deal with religion so that "the public" will be well served?

Any approach that speaks of "the public" in such broad terms can distort. To some, "the public" is an undifferentiated, monolithic mass; to others, it simply means "people," in all their variety; and to others still, it conjures up something like "the majority," suppressing the interests of minorities and eliminating curiosity about anything not considered "mainstream." Consequently, one must be cautious about any reference to an undefined "public," and for the sake of advancing the conversation on this subject, we need to do some examining.

We will present the issue in thesis form, designed to stimulate curiosity and reaction. This thesis will hold that the United States is made up of a mass known as "the public" and any number of intersecting "subpublics."

Some people who approach our topic would despair of finding any curricular tracks that do justice to the people as a single public who together make up one national society. Often these critics concentrate on the concept of a canon. They regard the choice of texts by those who teach or publicize, in this case religious texts, as a biasing activity. The choices made reflect what the dominant cultural leadership wants to have regarded as standard and normative. Thus an "American" canon would privilege Christian over Jewish, Jewish over Muslim, and all three faith traditions over all others. Some in the academy may study the new religious movements using the tools of social scientific research. But the academy tends to be suspicious of and dismissive of "cults" and the people in them. Anything regarded as marginal gets relegated to realms beyond the standard public. So voodoo and witchcraft and healing movements will look eccentric to most scholars—even if they are mainstream for thousands of citizens, who also pay their taxes and want the best of their schools.

On a larger scale, public elements confront each other, off campus and on. Some Catholic "rights" groups look for traces of anti-Catholicism in higher academia and claim to see systematic discrimination. Jews today find it hard to recall the days when there were Jewish quotas at private schools and when antisemitism was considered a sign of sophistication—but even today, not everything observant Jews cherish is mainstream. Evangelicals claim that when the American story is put together or when badges of status get handed out, they are often slighted and even disdained by lofty academics.

Mention those blocs and soon a whole series of resentments and charges arises. Where are Native American understandings of America and religion in all this? Gays and lesbians have formed interest groups and in many places have promoted historical and other studies of homosexuality. Very little in the existing canon favors inquiry about such matters. Does this mean that these groups should be ruled out of "the public"? Religious, ethnic, racial, economic, aesthetic, and other groups are made up of people who are fellow citizens but do not see themselves as responsible for or included in most concepts of "the public." And the university is their main forum for expressing the interests of their identity groups.

Without question, much of the criticism from these groups has been warranted and telling. A few hours with the textbooks of the past, a semester-long study of the canons of American history and social sciences, a canvass of how power in America has been bartered—all these would confirm the presence of biases implanted by the elites who for decades and centuries "ran" the culture.

At the same time, many of the points that come from what we are calling subpublics have by now been made. In American religious historical studies, for example, there is now less curiosity and attention paid to the old male Protestant mainstream than to feminist, non-Western, and formerly "marginal" and "outsider" concerns. Picture academics trying to get a hearing for John Wesley or John Calvin and their contemporary exponents in any way comparable to the audiences that would be attracted to campus appearances by African American leaders, gay and lesbian spokespersons, or proponents of occult and esoteric religions. By the laws of compensation, things are working out reasonably well.

Instead of trying to settle this issue of competitive publics in advance, it would be more profitable to study the interaction among subpublics and between the various subpublics and the general public. The student of religion has something particular to offer on this front. On one hand, religion is highly particularized, appropriated in thousands of groups, many of them mutually contradictory in their assertions and each of them following particular tracks in truth claims, worship, and practices. On the other hand, they do generate a set of concerns that are so widely influential that they come near to being universal. Religious interests by definition call people to take some control of their destiny. They belong to and are saved and impelled by a group—though individual religion is also strong and growing—but they must still believe for themselves as they must die for themselves. Yet their interests converge.

In Peter Burke's *Varieties of Cultural History*, the author jumbled together terms suggesting the ways in which cultural forces—here including religion—overlap and intersect. No one and nothing remains pure. Burke assembled a playful jumble of jargon for our enjoyment and learning. He spoke of "the processes of cultural borrowing, appropriation, exchange, reception, transfer, negotiation, resistance, syncretism, acculturation, enculturation, inculturation, interculturation, transculturation, hybridization (*mestizaje*), creolization, and the interaction and interpenetration of cultures." He notes that some Spanish scholars "now speak of '*mudejarism*' in their cultural history." These and other concepts "reveal a new conception of culture as *bricolage*, in which the process of appropriation and assimilation is not marginal but central."[1] These words look alienating when taken singly and overwhelming when run together. Yet Burke is not interested in having each pondered separately. Their sequential appearance is an example of the medium being the message. The point is merely that there are many words for mingling cultural elements in a general public.

The message is that pluralist and multicultural America, with its subpublics, also creates another kind of public in which certain common terms and expressions develop. Of course, America may indeed be in the throes of what many consider a "culture war." And of course, America sees profound and apparently irreparable schisms among the separate groups and subpublics, just as there are divisions over basic issues in the culture.

But at the same time, as in so many matters of opinion and modes of practice, there are also convergences. The Constitution regularly gets tested and yet retains its place. The affirmations of the Declaration of Independence receive more than lip service. There may be no single grand narrative that holds everyone together, but the public clearly cherishes narratives that edify and illuminate the nation. If John Winthrop and the Puritans progressively slip from public consciousness because they do not explain enough of America—a debatable point on its own terms—civil rights leaders like Martin Luther King Jr. become uniting points, as do figures in other movements.

Nine out of ten Americans say they believe in God. Those who worship do so under the cover of an astonishing variety of practices. But they also slip progressively into familiar patterns and consequently seem ever less threatening to each other. Yes, there are militias and Klans and other excrescences that one expects to see in a free society of 275 million people. Yet even the more mainstream Christian Right likes to speak of and seek "coalitions" and "majorities" and wants to "win it all," which means to gain dominance through a major political party, while others build overlapping coalitional constituencies.

Enter a Buddhist temple in a city with a large Asian population and the differences between this religion and, say, Christianity will at once be apparent. Yet the congregation—a non-Buddhist concept itself—will also have acquired dimensions of practice that conform to old Protestant patterns. In some cases, one finds pews and organs and Sunday bulletins and offering envelopes and fund drives and committees. All of these are alien to the ways of Japan or Thailand but almost self-evidently necessary in the American pattern.

Similarly, African American spirituals make their way into high-church "white" church worship, just as blacks borrowed and develop denominational patterns from whites. People adhere to both generalizing civil religion with its claims on one hand and to highly particular church religion with its sometimes contradictory challenges to the civic faith.

A few groups work—strenuously, it is true—to stay out of the admixtures. The Amish stand back from high school education and do not defend themselves in court. But then the American Civil Liberties Union takes their case and mainstreams their differences, so they remain legal by stretched definition, winning respect for the testimony their way of life offers. Others can and do withhold consent from the civic faith and turn critical of the nation's ways. But they suffer no civil penalties for doing so. They get tenure and publish through glossy magazines and come to be called prophets while they make profits from their critical literature that "only goes so far" but remains in the field of consensus. It is hard to escape from this zone of "interpenetration of cultures." Rather than try to shrug it off, the public university embodies it, wrestles with it, and seeks to influence the surrounding society about it.

Ask questions, as pollsters do, about ideas to which religion is relevant and where it had a shaping influence, and the responses rarely suggest that Americans have nothing in common. Almost all will argue that freedom and responsibility connect; that people should help the less fortunate; that family ties, however defined, are important; that the United States is the world's great nation; that spiritual and religious belief are essential in the nation; that the nonspiritual and nonreligious are at a disadvantage—one could extend the list considerably without running into a point of contention.

By bringing up this feature of American life, we are only suggesting that citizens have enough in common to create a public, as in a "public university," and that in religious studies at such places, the interaction itself can be a matter for research, argument, and different sets of relative resolutions in each generation.

In the America of fifty years ago, when its pluralism, religious and otherwise, was less recognized in the academy and the public sphere; when public order was in the hands of only one set of people; before the subpublics came to be visible and articulate, these questions were not asked with the intensity and regularity that they are asked today. Paradoxically, the more diverse America conceived itself to be and the more varieties of religious voices that were present, the easier it became to talk about it. Technically, there is far more to master in a pluralist society than in a homogeneous one, and no one can dream of mastering it in detail. But there is more need now to understand the other and the faith or nonfaith of the other, and there are more tools available and more locales in which to do the addressing than before.

Critics of the concept of public religion sometimes regard advocates of its expression as secret evangelists for faith communities. But if that were so, they should be accused of pursuing their calling very inefficiently. Other critics are from within faith communities. We have heard them saying, in effect, "Leave religion in its private box, and it will be purer than if it is exposed to the public arena," or, "Let the public sphere go its own way, ignoring the competing and often disturbing and unhelpful words and actions of religious programs," or, "Let religion fade and spirituality rule."

Our contention throughout this book, the theme that we are tossing on the table with the expectation that people will advance the conversation on several fronts, is this: in the midst of global, national, and local change affecting worldviews and public action, religion is too widespread and too deep a phenomenon *not* to be reckoned with in primary or at least secondary schools and thereafter, no matter under what aegis or auspices. To say this is to do no public relations favor to religion, because the disturbing sides of religion will be up for examination as much as the positive sides might be.

Though almost everyone who takes up the subject in education is likely to grow in understanding of the power religion holds in many guises, obscured as it is by other forces, not all will grow to appreciate religion more. They may find new reasons to resent its reach, to accuse its adherents of bad faith.

Those who favor one or another expression of religion have to take their risks with its exposure on the academic front. But they will have seen those who advocate study of it and who study it well to be servants of a public scene in which educators and educated alike will deal more fairly with the reality around them than they did when too readily the academy reduced our society to the conception of its being a simply secular one. Humans as individuals and in society are too full of passions, of intelligence, of mystery to be properly characterized as members of such a reduced society. To what they are tending, in their marvelous and contradictory ways, no one to my knowledge can envision or expound with authority. We'll have to study that for years to come. Which is why "public religion and education" on all levels is such a promising topic.

And it will fulfill more of its promise if citizens, whether responsible for schooling on any level or not, will probe the subjects and the thoughts and actions of each other as they "advance the conversation" for the common good. We expect that dealing with education and religion through the various stages of schooling will help them see the subject whole. They should also find new motivation to engage in such conversation and new means for advancing that common good. Thus they might even do their part in helping prevent a breakdown in American spiritual and political life. Figuratively, let us ring the bell, invite other citizens to the table, and urge them to join the conversation. Start talking!

Resources

Books

Several recent books tackle the topic of religion and education. Among them is James W. Fraser's *Between Church and State: Religion and Public Education in a Multicultural America* (New York: St. Martin's Press, 1999). In the interest of a "religiously tolerant and religiously informed America," Fraser argues that religion belongs in any truly multicultural educational curriculum. He surveys the American history of religion and public education and finally asks, "What's next?" His examination of some of the recent approaches to religion in education is followed by a brief but helpful list of sources for further reading.

Others have made equally persuasive cases for including religion in the curriculum. Nel Noddings argues for the positive role of public schools in *Educating for Intelligent Belief or Unbelief* (New York: Teachers College Press, 1993). While teachers must try to maintain pedagogical neutrality, Noddings contends, religious topics deserve serious treatment in the classroom in order to further students' moral, intellectual, and spiritual development. Critical thinking can best be taught by tackling, across the curriculum, the difficult questions of meaning and origins. Noddings provides a thoughtful and complete survey of those issues and the ways in which classrooms might creatively deal with them.

Warren A. Nord also makes a comprehensive case that public education, from early schooling through college, should take religion seriously. In *Religion and American Education: Rethinking a National Dilemma* (Chapel Hill: University of North Carolina Press, 1995), Nord points to a paradox: if we Americans are so religious, why does our educational system ignore religion? Ranging widely, the author combines philosophical, moral, and practical arguments for restoring the tension between religion and the secular in education. Nord ends by offering some specifics on what students should learn about religion.

Nord and colleague Charles C. Haynes offer advice in *Taking Religion Seriously Across the Curriculum* (Alexandria, Va.: Association for Supervision and Curriculum Development, 1998). After making the case for including religion in public education, the authors explore in detail the major issues associated with teaching religion in various areas of the elementary to high school curriculum, ranging from economics and science to history and sex education.

Moving beyond the argument for religion in public education, Robert J. Nash writes engagingly in *Faith, Hype, and Clarity: Teaching About Religion in American Schools and Colleges* (New York: Teachers College Press, 1999). Accepting the recent arguments of scholars such as Noddings and Nord, Nash moves to discuss the *what* and the *how* of dealing with religion in the classroom. He suggests dividing religious traditions into four types of narratives: fundamentalist, prophetic, alternative (neognostic) spiritualities, and posttheist. By examining these worldviews as different kinds of narratives, Nash suggests that through his instructional model, students can be led to understand more clearly the hermeneutical prisms of themselves and others.

Curriculum, Religion, and Public Education: Conversations for an Enlarging Public Square (New York: Teachers College Press, 1998) also offers a wealth of practical advice. Edited by James T. Sears with

James C. Carper, this volume allows listeners to eavesdrop on a wide variety of voices as they engage an equally wide range of issues. Part One details the historical and legal background for contemporary curricular debates. Part Two takes up, in detail, five curricular areas that have occasioned much debate: textbooks, values, sex education, outcome-based education, and science. In the last section, readers are treated to a series of "community dialogues" among educators, scholars, and other professionals as they consider the topics raised earlier in the book.

Several works take on the constitutional dimensions of religion in the schools. Charles Haynes, with coeditor Oliver Thomas, offers a detailed and user-friendly map of the terrain in *Finding Common Ground: A First Amendment Guide to Religion and Education* (Nashville, Tenn.: Freedom Forum First Amendment Center, 1994). With a clear, attractive, and easy-to-follow structure, this work provides practical tips and strategies for school leaders, parents, and concerned citizens in negotiating issues such as religious holidays, equal access, character education, and even how to structure productive civil discussions on the issues. One key strength of this volume is its guide to resources for teaching about the religious dimensions of American history, world religions, and character education. The book concludes with a helpful section on sample school district policies.

Case studies often provide insight into the dimensions of the conflict over religion in public schools. In *Secular Darkness: Religious Right Involvement in Texas Public Education, 1963–1989* (New York: Lang, 1995), James R. Durham describes how battles over the content of public school textbooks reveal the fault lines in contemporary debates over religion in education. Another fascinating tale is told by Stephen Bates in *Battleground: One Mother's Crusade, the Religious Right, and the Struggle for Control of Our Classrooms* (New York: Henry Holt, 1993). Recounting events in Church Hill, Tennessee, the author details how Vicki Frost's uneasiness with her second-grade daughter's schoolbooks blossomed into a full-blown skirmish in the culture wars, one that drew national resources and attention.

Scholars have spent a great deal of energy on the specific issue of school prayer. Interested readers could begin with the historically thorough *Should the Children Pray? A Historical, Judicial, and Political Examination of Public School Prayer* (Waco, Tex.: Markham Press Fund, 1989), by Lynda Beck Fenwick. Seeking a more clearheaded contemporary discussion, the author reexamines the history of prayer and religious freedom in the United States. Key historical moments include the colonial era, the *Engel* decision (early 1960s), and the mid-1980s, when efforts intensified to add a school prayer amendment to the Constitution. Other similar books include Robert S. Alley's *Without a Prayer: Religion Expression in the Public Schools* (Buffalo, N.Y.: Prometheus Books, 1996) and Tricia Andryszewski's *School Prayer: A History of the Debate* (Berkeley Heights, N.J.: Enslow, 1997).

Eugene F. Provenzo Jr. provides a comprehensive account of religious conservatives and public education in *Religious Fundamentalism and American Education: The Battle for the Public Schools* (Albany: State University of New York Press, 1990). In concise fashion, Provenzo details the impact of what he calls "Ultra-Fundamentalism" on public education. Convinced that American public education and culture has been corrupted by secular humanism, this movement has raised critical questions for public consideration: how public education forms students philosophically, the rightful realm of parental instruction, creationism, school prayer, censorship, textbooks, the family and education, and state regulation of private religious schools. While admitting the acuity of their criticism, Provenzo concludes that the ultra-fundamentalists make demands that are "ultimately inconsistent with the realities of American democracy." *School Wars: Resolving Our Conflicts over Religion and Values* (San Francisco: Jossey-Bass, 1996), by Barbara B. Gaddy,

T. William Hall, and Robert J. Marzano, takes up conservative religious challenges to public education. Concentrating on the variety of curricular locations where those challenges appear, the authors provide detailed, practical ways for negotiating conflicts between people with differing worldviews. Appendixes offer a variety of useful resources for educators, parents, and community leaders actively involved in this arena.

A unique and helpful volume is *Religion in the Schools: A Reference Handbook* (Santa Barbara, Calif.: ABC-CLIO, 1998), by James John Jurinski. Part of the Contemporary World Issues series, this work combines several helpful resources: a historical chronology from 1620 to 1998, biographical sketches of important figures, primary documents, excerpts from court cases, quotations, examinations of six "key conflict areas," a directory of organizations and associations, a glossary of key terms, and a list of both print and nonprint resources, including videos and Internet sites.

Giving attention to the specifically Catholic dimensions of religion and education, Philip Gleason has written *Contending with Modernity: Catholic Higher Education in the Twentieth Century* (New York: Oxford University Press, 1995). Gleason, in the first synthetic developmental account of this subject, pays special attention to the institutional and intellectual dimensions of this history. An older but also useful volume is *Catholic School Education in the United States: Development and Current Concerns* (New York: Garland, 1992), by Mary A. Grant and Thomas C. Hunt. In addition to providing a general history from colonial times through the post–Vatican II era, the authors provide detailed bibliographic entries. In *Religion and the Public Schools in 19th Century America: The Contribution of Orestes A. Brownson* (Mahwah, N.J.: Paulist Press, 1996), Edward J. Power provides a thorough intellectual account of the educational theories of Orestes Brownson, an influential lay Catholic apologist and champion of the compatibility between Catholicism and democracy.

Many recent works treat religion and higher education in the United States. For the early story, turn to Robert S. Shepard, *God's People in the Ivory Tower: Religion in the Early American University* (Brooklyn: Carlson, 1991).

In *The Soul of the American University: From Protestant Establishment to Established Nonbelief* (New York: Oxford University Press, 1994), George M. Marsden tells the story of the transformation of major American universities from generally religious to mostly secular institutions. While admitting that this educational disestablishment of religion may have been positive, Marsden notes that these schools have in fact become so hostile toward religion that they unfairly exclude religious viewpoints. Marsden further develops his argument for including religious viewpoints in university education in *The Outrageous Idea of Christian Scholarship* (New York: Oxford University Press, 1997). An earlier volume, edited by Marsden and Bradley J. Longfield, *The Secularization of the Academy* (New York: Oxford University Press, 1992), provides various essays on topics from Catholic education in the twentieth century to higher education in Britain and Canada.

In *The Dying of the Light: The Disengagement of Colleges and Universities from Their Christian Churches* (Grand Rapids, Mich.: Eerdmans, 1998), James T. Burtchaell shows how seventeen American colleges and universities founded by Protestant denominations slowly abandoned their religious roots in order to accommodate prevailing secular standards of knowledge. D. G. Hart, in *The University Gets Religion: Religious Studies in American Higher Education* (Baltimore: Johns Hopkins University Press, 1999), traces the rise of religion as an important academic discipline since World War II. Hart contends that although Protestantism has been successful in securing a place for the academic study of religion in higher education, religion no longer possesses a coherent justification for its existence as a discipline because it has become so diverse. Perhaps, Hart suggests, a religion-friendly university is not the blessing that scholars of religion seek.

Electronic Resources

Many electronic resources on religion and education are available. The president's guidelines on Religion in the Public Schools can be viewed and downloaded at the Department of Education's Web site: *www.ed.gov/inits/religionandschools*. This site also provides other guidelines specifically tailored for parents, teachers, and community organizations.

For accounts of contemporary church-state conflicts, including those in education, readers can turn to the comprehensive resources of the Freedom Forum. This organization keeps abreast of recent events, offers in-depth examinations of particular issues such as school vouchers, analyzes court decisions, and provides links to other relevant resources. Some topical publications are also available to download. Begin exploring at *www.freedomforum.org/religion*.

Many organizations actively participate in debates over religion and education. Among them is the Rutherford Institute, a nonprofit Christian legal foundation dedicated to preserving religious rights in public forums. The Web site is at *www.rutherford.org*, where a variety of resources are available. See also founder John W. Whitehead's *Rights of Religious Persons in Public Education* (Wheaton, Ill.: Crossway Books, 1994). Similar organizations include the American Center for Law and Justice (*www.aclj.org*) and the Becket Fund for Religious Liberty (*www.becketfund.org*).

Also numerous are groups that contend for a stricter understanding of the separation of church and state. The "Religious Liberty" section of the American Civil Liberties Union can be found at *www.aclu.org/issues/religion/hmrf.html*, which includes a short list of links to other relevant sites. The always active Americans United for Separation of Church and State is accessible at *www.au.org*. People for the American Way maintains sections titled "About the Religious Right" and "Religious Liberty" at *www.pfaw.org/issues*.

Notes

Chapter Two

1. I used a similar exercise in Martin E. Marty and R. Scott Appleby, *The Glory and the Power: The Fundamentalist Challenge to the Modern World* (Boston: Beacon Press, 1992).

2. Thomas Luckmann, *The Invisible Religion: The Problem of Religion in Modern Society* (Old Tappan, N.J.: Macmillan, 1967).

3. Ernest Gellner, *Conditions of Liberty: Civil Society and Its Rivals* (New York, Penguin, 1994), pp. 97–100.

Chapter Three

1. Crane Brinton, quoted in Sidney E. Mead, *The Nation with the Soul of a Church* (New York: HarperCollins, 1975), p. 118.

2. For example, Thomas Paine wrote, "My own mind is my own church," in *The Age of Reason* (1794), p. 1.

3. J. Paul Williams, *The New Education and Religion: A Challenge to Secularism in Education* (New York: Association Press, 1945); J. Paul Williams, *What Americans Believe and How They Worship* (New York: HarperCollins, 1962).

4. Will Herberg, *Protestant-Catholic-Jew: An Essay in American Religious Sociology* (New York: Doubleday, 1955).

5. Robert N. Bellah, "Civil Religion in America," *Daedalus*, Winter 1967, pp. 1–21.

Chapter Four

1. Philip W. Jackson, Robert E. Boostrom, and David T. Hansen, *The Moral Life of Schools* (San Francisco: Jossey-Bass, 1993).

2. Ibid., p. 4.

3. Ibid., pp. 4–6.

4. Ibid., p. 7.

5. Ibid., pp. 295–311.

6. Basil Mitchell, *Morality, Religious and Secular: The Dilemma of the Traditional Conscience* (Oxford: Clarendon Press, 1980).

Chapter Six

1. See, for example, Paul Blanshard, *American Freedom and Catholic Power* (Boston: Beacon Press, 1949).

2. James G. Dwyer, *Religious Schools v. Children's Rights* (Ithaca, N.Y.: Cornell University Press, 1998).

3. Ibid.

4. Ibid., pp. 180–182.

5. John Tracy Ellis, *American Catholicism*, 2d ed. rev. (Chicago: University of Chicago Press, 1969), p. 139.

Chapter Seven

1. James T. Burtchaell, *The Dying of the Light: The Disengagement of Colleges and Universities from Their Christian Churches* (Grand Rapids, Mich.: Eerdmans, 1998).

2. George M. Marsden, *The Soul of the American University: From Protestant Establishment to Established Nonbelief* (New York: Oxford University Press, 1994).

3. Gabriel Marcel, *Creative Fidelity*, trans. Robert Rosthal (New York: Farrar, Strauss & Giroux, 1964).

4. W. H. Auden, "New Year Letter (January 1, 1940)," in *Collected Poems*, ed. Edward Mendelsohn (New York: Random House, 1976), p. 179.

Chapter Eight

1. John Dewey, "From Absolutism to Experimentalism," in George P. Adams and William P. Montague (eds.), *Contemporary American Philosophy*, Vol. 2 (Old Tappan, N.J.: Macmillan, 1930), p. 19.

Chapter Nine

1. Alfred Schutz, *Reflections on the Problem of Relevance* (New Haven, Conn.: Yale University Press, 1970).

Chapter Ten

1. Peter Burke, *Varieties of Cultural History* (Ithaca, N.Y.: Cornell University Press, 1997), p. 208.

The Author

M artin E. Marty, the Fairfax M. Cone Distinguished Service
Professor Emeritus at the University of Chicago, directed the
three-year Public Religion Project for The Pew Charitable Trusts.
Author of more than fifty books and winner of the National Book
Award for *Righteous Empire*, Marty coedited five volumes for the
Fundamentalism Project. He is also a recipient of the National
Humanities Medal. An ordained minister, Marty served for a decade
as a Lutheran pastor before joining the University of Chicago fac-
ulty, where he taught for thirty-five years.

Jonathan Moore is a Ph.D. candidate in the history of Christianity
at the University of Chicago Divinity School. His current research
examines evangelicalism and church-state conflicts in contemporary America.

About the Public Religion Project

This book is a product of Public Religion Project–sponsored conversations on public religion and education. The Public Religion Project, a three-year endeavor (1996–1999) funded by The Pew Charitable Trusts and hosted by the University of Chicago, held these conversations as part of its assignment to "promote efforts to bring to light and interpret the forces of faith within a pluralistic society."

This charter called on the project to find ways to help ensure that religion in its many voices was well represented in North American public life; to bring to the fore often neglected resources for healing of body, mind, spirit, and public life that religion manifests; to work to clarify the roles of religion in public spheres by engaging various expressions of faith, even those that are repressive or destructive; and to lift up situations in which dialogue, mutual respect, and the search for common values and solutions have successfully proceeded.

In these pursuits, the project did not line up with partisans in "culture wars" or ideological conflicts. Certainly, the project was "pro-publicness," contending that American society is better off when it is aware of the religious forces and voices, and thus it worked to enhance this concept of "public" religion while honoring the private and communal energizing sources and outlets of people of faith.

In its undertakings, the project considered ten zones of public life where forces of faith are at work. One of these was education. In hosting the series of conversations on this topic, the project invited educators and administrators from elementary and secondary levels, private colleges, and public universities, as well as scholars of education—all with a keen interest in religion—to the table. This book reflects the voices and concerns heard around that table.

I've often compared the project's work to that of atomic accelerators or jet propulsion laboratories: it took objects, events, energies, and forces already extant and active and set out to propel them into new areas. We hope this conversation, begun around our table and now continued with you, will be part of that dynamic.

Index